Scientific Management
of
Library Operations

by

Richard M. Dougherty
and
Fred. J. Heinritz

The Scarecrow Press, Inc.
New York and London   1966

To
Carole
and
my
parents

To
my
mother
and
father

Preface

Scientific management principles and techniques have not been entirely ignored by the library profession. A few hardy pioneers such as Fremont Rider, Joseph Wheeler, and Ralph Shaw have tried persistently to awaken librarian's interest in this subject. However, there is still not general recognition and acceptance among librarians that, although the foundationstone of librarianship is bibliography, the profession also includes many elements common to business and industry. Business executives and industrial engineers have long known the value of scientific management.

Interest in scientific management has been stimulated by the advent of data processing methods. Any library that intends to convert its operations to automatic equipment must first examine, in minute detail, its present methods. One of the glaring faults with some of the current efforts to automate has been the failure to examine and evaluate adequately present practices and objectives. As a result the automated system, based on an inefficient manual system, proves cumbersome and overly expensive.

Over the years many texts dealing with motion and time study, work measurement, and work simplification have appeared in print. However, no book which presents the principles and techniques of scientific management as they apply specifically to library oriented problems is presently available. The need for such a volume has been impressed forceably upon the authors by their teaching of courses on library operations in library schools. This book is intended both as a textbook for library school students and a handbook for practicing librarians. It will acquaint the former with the basic tools of the management analyst and will aid the latter in improving their present systems. The major analysis techniques are described in step-by-step detail, with a wealth of illustrations and library examples.

v

The authors are deeply grateful to the many individuals who have contributed to the writing of this book. They are particularly grateful to Miss Viola Maihl, Director of the Linden, New Jersey Public Library, who graciously consented to allow them to use the Linden Library as a laboratory and to include the findings of a study conducted in the library a few years ago, in order to present an illustrative case study in depth.

The authors are also grateful to Mr. Kwok-Ying Fung, who doubles as a full-time school librarian in Norwalk, Connecticut and as a part-time professional photographer, and to Mr. Samuel Boone, Chief of the Library's Photo-Reproduction Section at the University of North Carolina at Chapel Hill. Mr. Fung is responsible for the following photographs: 5:6, 7; 12:3-20, 22-28, 30-37; and 13:1. Mr. Boone is responsible for 5:4; 6:4-12; 8:1; and 10:2.

The authors also wish to express their appreciation to Meylan Stopwatch Corp., Keuffel & Esser Co., International Business Machines Corp., Stanford University Press, The Royal Statistical Society, Stamats Publishing Co., and the Graduate School of Library Service of Rutgers University for the use of their materials. The illustrative material furnished by these organizations made a significant contribution to the text.

The authors also wish to thank Mr. Ashby Fristoe and Miss Beatrice Montgomery who proofread the manuscript and also provided critical comments. Finally, the authors wish to thank the four typists, Mrs. Joann Huntington, Mrs. Carol Swaine, Miss Ann Puckett, and Miss Gary Luttrell, who in some instances performed this work in addition to their regular duties.

Richard M. Dougherty
Fred J. Heinritz

Contents

Chapter I
Scientific Management: What It Is and Is Not

The high-sounding term Scientific Management
should not be allowed to mislead anybody. It
is not something that can be bought wholesale
and utilized retail, but simply means: Study
your problem according to scientific methods,
eliminating guess, setting each man a proper
task, and allowing suitable rewards for the accomplishment of these tasks. This done, increased efficiency is bound to follow.
- Henry L. Gantt (1911)

Definition and History of Scientific Management

Scientific management is the application of the principles
and methodology of modern science to problems of administration.
Most of us are familiar with the principles and methods of modern
science, for, even if we might not be able to articulate them at an
instant's notice, we have absorbed them willy-nilly in the process
of growing up in twentieth-century America. The great break of
modern science with the past is summed up succinctly by the motto
of the Royal Society of London: Nothing on faith. If you want me
to accept your view, prove that it's better than mine. I insist on
evidence that is mensurable. How we "do it good" in our libraries,
or our unsubstantiated opinion about how to "do it good" are usually
interesting and sometimes useful, but our opinions are not in themselves proof that how we operate, or think we might, is the most
efficient or otherwise desirable procedure. The basic methodology
of science is the study or experiment. The method for making a
scientific management study is covered in detail in Chapter II.

The principles and methods of modern science have con-

13

sistently proven their worth ever since they began to come into
vogue in the seventeenth century.   Their first major application was
to the material world of mass, force, energy, light -- those items
now grouped loosely under the term physical science.   The industrial revolution was not slow to adapt this knowledge to its needs.
The astonishing success of this approach to the physical world is
so much a part of the fabric of our daily lives as to need no elab-
oration here.   A natural consequence of this success with the physical world was the attempt to extend the application of scientific
principles and methods to life -- to plants, animals, man, and man
in his social relations.   In such areas as medicine and agriculture,
this attempt has been extraordinarily successful.   However, with
regard to man in his social relations, positive results, although
they both can be and are obtained, are to date less sudden and certain.

        Thus it is not surprising that when an attempt was made in
the early twentieth century to study human organization scientifically there was both a temptation and tendency to emphasize its physical aspects at the expense of human relations.   The American pioneers of the movement to study industrial organization scientifically
recognized this danger, and spoke out against it.   However, the immediate, tangible gains of this new approach for many years impressed the public more than the admonitions.   As labor became
better organized within itself, and hence a potent bargaining force,
and as research and experience increased our psychological sophis-
tication, the human side of management came more to the fore and
began to receive its due.   The famed Hawthorne Experiments, carried out at the Hawthorne Works of the Western Electric Company
from 1927 to 1932, are usually cited as being particularly influen-
tial in exploding the notion that the worker's only concern was his
pay check, and proving that individual and group motivation had an
important influence upon productivity.   The heart of scientific management remains scientific study of the physical aspects of human
organization, but modern scientific management operates within the
framework of individual and social needs and aspirations.   It has
to -- society will otherwise no longer tolerate it.

Although he did have predecessors, Frederick Taylor (1856-1915), is generally credited as being the father of scientific management. Taylor believed that the casual, rule-of-thumb approach to management prevalent in his day should be replaced by scientific analysis. He developed a number of management principles which are still applicable. Among his contributions was the scientific development of time study and standards. He tried to decide what constituted a fair day's work on the basis of an extensive study of a particular job, rather than by means of a supervisor's offhand estimate, or the least amount of work an employee thought he could get by doing. Taylor's closest associates were Carl Barth, Horace Hathaway, Morris Cooke, and Henry Gantt. Gantt pioneered in developing techniques for planning and scheduling work (the Gantt chart is still in use) and is noted as one of the earliest scientific management men in America to direct his major interest to the human being in industry. Frank (1868-1924) and Lillian (1878-   ) Gilbreth, who have achieved incidental immortality via the bestselling book and movie, ''Cheaper by the Dozen,'' rank with Taylor as contributors to the development of scientific management. The Gilbreths became interested in motion economy -- the elimination of nonproductive body motions. For their studies they devised and developed the flow process chart. The varied activities of the Gilbreths included noteworthy inventions and improvements in building and construction work and the development of such techniques as micromotion study by means of motion pictures.

Scientific management began in industry, and only later was applied to public administration and services. It is difficult to discern from the literature exactly when librarians began to analyze library routines scientifically. It seems safe to assume that some librarians have always used scientific management (whatever the label attached), but that many more have not. It is significant to note, however, that in recent years, more interest in scientific management has manifested itself within the profession. For further reading on the history of scientific management, the reader is referred to the bibliography at the end of this chapter.

Value of Scientific Management to Librarians

Few persons have difficulty in understanding -- at least in theory -- the value of scientific management to industry. Scientific management (as opposed to unscientific management) improves production and distribution efficiency. This decreases production costs and distribution costs and allows the product to be sold for less. This in turn enables industry, by selling more items because the price is lower, to increase profits. Increased profits make possible larger dividends for stockholders, and larger salaries for both management and labor.

Libraries, however, do not operate for the purpose of financial profit. Thus it has been argued by some librarians that scientific management need not be applied to them. This is a fallacious notion. The very fact that libraries are not dependent upon showing a financial profit in order to exist makes it even more imperative that they be well-managed. It might be difficult for a librarian, who can normally expect at least subsistence from the local exchequer, and who has little management training, to be as deeply efficiency conscious as an industrial manager whose career hangs on the result of each succeeding balance sheet. Dollars are easier to measure than service.

Libraries share with the multitude of other governmental and public service organizations in any community the responsibility for giving the taxpayer a maximum return of service for each dollar invested. As tax rates continue to spiral upward, there is a louder clamor for agencies "feeding at the public trough" to justify their existence. There is evidence that the squeeze has already taken hold in some communities. Library bond issues have been defeated; school budgets are coming under closer scrutiny and questioning by increasingly alarmed property owners. Under these conditions, if scientific management will help a librarian demonstrate operational efficiency, then he should be professionally obligated to make use of it. When a librarian requests more money for his library, the men in charge of dispensing funds want to know why the increase is needed. Scientific management will help in developing a factual ar-

gument for the additional funds.   Experienced appropriating com-
mittees are, by and large, more impressed by a quantitative, factual justification than by panegyrics on librarianship.

No librarian desires that the taxpayer receive less than maximum return on his library investment.   Some librarians do, however, question that scientific management is an aid to this end.
They argue that library work does not lend itself to scientific analysis.   How, they say, can such activities as the judgment brought
to bear in book selection, the quality of reference service, or the
beneficial influence of a library on a user and a community be
measured?   In answer it must be admitted that these library phe-
nomena, as well as others of a similar nature, are difficult to
measure.   However, it is also fair to add that, despite their complexity, and the large number of variables involved, these phenom-
ena are with effort amenable to usefully accurate measurement, and
that our ability to make such measurements is steadily improving.
The difference between this sort of measurement and, for instance,
measuring the number of cards in a catalog is one of degree of
complexity, rather than kind.

This argument against the efficacy of scientific management
in libraries disregards the very substantial part of library work
that consists of repetitive, mechanical routines that lend themselves
readily to quantitative analysis.   In terms of total hours required
for performance, the largest bulk of library work -- perhaps as
much as 70 to 90% of all current library tasks -- consists of such
routines.   Upon analyzing a process such as ordering, cataloging,
card filing, binding, circulation, or shelving into its constituent
steps, it is apparent that, although some jobs are less clearly mechanical than others, and that now and then there may be a job that
is not fairly called mechanical at all, the majority of tasks are in
essence quite repetitive and measurable.

In addition to improving routine efficiency, scientific management is a useful tool of library personnel management and financial
administration.   Work analysis is the key to modern job classification.   Only when we have ascertained of what the job consists, and
what level of productivity we may reasonably expect of the person

performing it, are we able to define intelligently what sort of in-
nate ability and special training are necessary for its performance.

Frequently the benefits of scientific management to the profession or to an institution are emphasized, but the value of management
to individuals who (with or without formal training) can apply management principles to their daily work are overlooked. It is not difficult
for a person to improve his production by simple improvements such
as rearrangement of a work area, altering the sequence of steps for
performing a job, or by batching work instead of performing each cycle
as a unit. It is not unusual to find a worker, frequently an old-timer,
who seemingly produces infinite quantities of work without any notice-
able effort. Almost without exception, if one were to study these individuals he would find that in one way or another they have adopted numerous labor-saving, time-saving, common-sense shortcuts. In addition to personal satisfaction, it is not unreasonable to expect that in
time superior productivity will give a worker precedence in matters of
salary and promotion. Finally, when a worker himself becomes a supervisor, he will be better qualified to supervise if he is versed in
the fundamentals of scientific management.

Misconceptions About Scientific Management

Misuse of scientific management in the early decades of its
development has brought upon it unjustified opprobrium. Labor's
opposition to it was so vehement as to force Taylor in 1912 to de-
fend his views in hearings before a special committee of the House
of Representatives. Taylor's idea was to establish what amount of
production constituted a "fair day's work" by actually studying the
worker on the job and then to pay the worker who achieved this
standard a bonus. Those who did not achieve the established standard were not paid the bonus, but were paid a living wage. The
idea was not to exploit the laborer by working him to exhaustion,
but to encourage steady achievement at a reasonable pace that could
be kept up day after day without injury to health. Taylor thus felt
that management and labor shared in the responsibility of production, the former by establishing fair standards and planning the
work, and the latter by achieving the standards.

Unfortunately, some industrialists were less idealistic than Taylor, and saw in his idea of standards not so much an opportunity for labor and management cooperation as a chance to take advantage of the then relatively unorganized labor force. Workers who could produce at the reasonable rate sufficient to earn their bonus found that their standards were raised, and when the new level of production was attained, the bonus rate was again increased. It did not take workers long to view all time and motion men with a certain amount of mistrust -- mistrust which eventually gave rise to worker slowdowns. It should be noted, however, that the root of the trouble was not scientific management, but rather its abuse at the hands of unscrupulous individuals. Fire, depending on how it is used, can either cook our dinner and warm our toes, or burn down our house. Hopefully, the day of management speed-ups and labor slow-downs is past. The purpose of scientific management is to increase productivity without increasing effort, or, ideally to increase productivity while decreasing effort.

On the other hand, scientific management is not a panacea. It is not an end in itself. It is a proven tool that, when used intelligently, can aid library administrators in achieving the objectives of their libraries. However, in the quest to attain operational efficiency, we must not forget that cost is not the sole criterion of excellence. Quality of services must not be governed on the basis of cost alone. Our objective is to provide a service as economically as possible at the level of quality required. The remainder of this book is devoted to explaining in a specific manner how this tool, long a fixture in industry, can be applied also to aid in the solution of library problems.

Bibliography

General
Heyel, Carl, ed. The Encyclopedia of Management. New York: Reinhold, 1963.

See the articles on Scientific Management, Hawthorne Experiments, Taylor, Gilbreth, Gantt, etc. Includes References cited, Information, References, and Cross-References to other pertinent articles in the volume.

Merrill, Harwood F. , ed.   Classics in Management.   New York:
    American Management Association, 1960.

    Non-technical sections from the writings of fifteen manage-
    ment pioneers, including Taylor, Gibreth, and Gantt.   In-
    cludes selected bibliography of the writings of each man.

Taylor, Frederick W.   Scientific Management, Comprising Shop
    Management, The Principles of Scientific Management, Testi-
    mony Before the Special House Committee, with a foreword
    by Harlow S. Person.   New York: Harper, 1947.

    Three volumes in one.   Principles and Testimony are writ-
    ten for the layman; Shop Management is more technical.

Urwick, Lyndall, ed.   The Golden Book of Management, ed.   for
    the International Committee on Scientific Management (CIOS).
    London: Newman, 1956.

    Lists the major personalities in the modern management
    movement.   For each one includes a portrait, a summary of
    his career, a note on his personal characteristics, and a
    bibliography of his significant writings.

Libraries

Shaw, Ralph, ed.   "Scientific Management in Libraries," Library
    Trends, II, No. 2 (January, 1954).

    The most complete survey of the subject to date.   Includes
    bibliographies.

Chapter II
Making a Management Study

Why a Librarian Should Know How to Make a Management Study

Some librarians reading this chapter will undoubtedly conduct a management study at one time or another in their careers; others may never be called upon actually to perform one. Even if not, a librarian may become involved with studies in other ways. As an administrator he may find it necessary to decide when and if a study is appropriate, who should carry it out, and how to make best use of the results. He may also find himself one of the persons being studied. A knowledge of what is involved should make this a more rewarding experience and him a more cooperative subject. Finally, it is to be hoped that by learning how to make such a study, librarians will be encouraged to try their hand at it; and that knowledge of proper procedure as well as the pitfalls will enhance chances of success.

Who Should Make the Study

Ideally the person who undertakes a library management study should have some knowledge both of scientific management and of librarianship. But those possessing these credentials are still extremely scarce. In the beginning the usual practice was to rely on consultant firms from business and industry. Business-oriented consultants could not be expected to be as suited to evaluate library routines as a competent library-trained person. All too often, routines were studied in relation to costs alone. Service objectives were either subordinated or completely ignored. As a result, some of the pioneer management studies were a disappointment to librarians. Some management firms have conscientiously worked to overcome this initial shortcoming. In the meantime, more and more librarians are becoming management-oriented. Both developments are highly beneficial to the profession.

Any outside consultant, library-trained or not, can, by the sheer fact that he is an outsider, bring a fresh look to bear on a problem. He can often afford to speak more candidly of what is not as it should be than internal personnel who perhaps see the problems as clearly as he, but refrain from speaking for fear of losing their jobs or friends. In some cases, specialists are more than worth their fees.

Some larger libraries and library systems have one or more trained library specialists on their staff but most libraries do not have the funds to hire a full-time specialist. The creation of a special staff position for management study, as opposed to hiring an outside consultant, has the advantage of facilitating adequate follow-through after the study has been performed. Additionally, it can protect line administrators from imbroglios that can spring from unpopular findings and recommendations. The management analyst is performing as a staff officer in an advisory capacity.

The majority of library studies can (and should) be performed by a competent librarian with only a grounding in scientific management principles. In fact, today most studies are performed by practicing librarians -- sometimes by department heads, sometimes by individuals with no administrative responsibility. This is a healthy situation, and hopefully, as more librarians become management-oriented, the need for outside consultants or specialists will diminish.

Selecting an Area for Study
Frequently Performed Jobs

Since the time, money, or energy are not available to study everything and everybody, our efforts must be concentrated upon areas that are likely to yield the highest return for our study investment. The more frequently an operation is performed, the better a candidate it is for analysis. The reason for this is that even if we are able through improvements to save only a small amount of time each time the operation is performed, this saving multiplied by the high frequency makes the total time saved substantial. For example, suppose a library orders 10,000 books a year; suppose further that by some simple work flow improvement we are able to reduce the average time needed for some step in the ordering by one minute per book. This will produce an annual saving of 10,000 minutes or 167 hours, or a month's labor by a full-time employee each year. Searching, typing book orders, classifying and cuttering books, reproducing cards, filing cards, charging and discharging books, and shelving are obvious examples of high-frequency processes. In contrast, such a process as expanding the card catalog is necessary only now and then. Although even here a study prior to the actual move will no doubt save some time and expense, study of some more frequently performed process would probably save more.

Repetitious Jobs

The more repetitious a job, the more it lends itself to analysis. By repetitious is meant that steps recur each time that the job is performed. Book charging and discharging are examples of tasks that are typically repetitious.

Jobs Requiring Frequent Movement of People or Equipment

Tasks involving any considerable amount of movement of people or materials from one point to another are usually productive areas for study. The movement meant here is not necessarily that between two distant points. Short distances multiplied by high frequency equal long distances. Materials and equipment needed for any task that can be completed in one place should be located in that area. Placement of related library routines should be such as to reflect the natural flow of the work and thereby minimize the total steps. The increase of a few steps for a few persons might save many steps for many other persons. This sort of analysis is inseparably tied to the study of functional library architecture. What is the optimum physical arrangement between acquisitions, cataloging, reference, the public catalog, and the major bibliographic tools? One must analyze such factors as who on the library staff uses the public catalog? How often? How far do they have to travel to use it? How long does each trip to and from it take? And so on.

Jobs With Bottlenecks

　　Bottlenecks in any procedures should always receive prompt attention. A breakdown in even a seemingly minor link in the work-flow chain is a serious matter. For example, getting call numbers stamped or inked on the spine of a book is a mechanical, sub-professional task. It is, nonetheless, a necessary prerequisite to circulating a book. To the user it is just as serious if the delay is in labelling as in the professional task of cataloging, for in either case he has to wait. He just wants to use the book.

Jobs That Involve Large Amounts of Money

　　Finally, a job costing a large amount of money is an obvious area to select for study. High cost alone is of course no proper excuse in itself for eliminating or even partially curtailing an operation. Providing reference service in a large library is expensive; yet how many are actually campaigning for its curtailment or elimination? It is reasonable, however, to seek ways to reduce this high cost without reducing the service rendered. To take a case, some libraries, upon analyzing their reference questions, have discovered that the majority of questions asked by their patrons are directional and do not require a professionally trained librarian to answer them. Thus it is possible without lowering quality of service to utilize at the reference desk less costly personnel with little or no professional training for these. They are required to refer those questions they can not handle to the professional librarian in charge, who can concentrate on professional work.

Defining the Problem

　　It is not possible to define intelligently the scope of a study except in relation to the overall objectives of a total library system. As these objectives change, so must the study criteria. For example, in recent years the profession's emphasis has tended to shift from the organization to the use of library materials. If the reader's needs are considered paramount, then one is obligated to evaluate a system's efficiency in terms of its ability to satisfy those needs. All else is superfluous. Thus a library that is ap-

parently able to organize its collection efficiently is not helping the
reader if it is not organizing those materials which the reader
needs, or is not organizing the material in such a manner that it
is useful to the reader. Again, if reader needs are considered
paramount, efficient acquisition of materials at a rate many times
exceeding the capacity of the preparations departments to handle the
load might suggest that the library's objectives are not being met
because the reader's needs cannot be satisfied until the book is
ready for his use. The basic principle is that whether a study en-
compasses either a single library routine or an entire library, it
cannot afford to ignore the objectives and interactions of the entire
system.

One common mistake in the systems approach is to forget
"make-ready" (preparation) and "put-away" (clean-up) steps. For
many jobs, the time expended on these is (relatively insignificant;
however, for some jobs, it can become very important. To take a
case, an organization printed about 1475 pieces of card stock per
day. When in operation, the offset press printed about 100 pieces
of stock per minute. The actual press running time per day was
about 15 minutes, but the operation required close to an hour a day.
This was not because the pressman was incompetent. Assuming
the masters were already made, he still had to prepare the press
for each day's run. The rollers had to be inked, fountain solution
had to be poured, and the card stock had to be divested of its wrap-
pings and placed in position on the press. Then each master (there
were 20 different ones each day) had to be wiped over with "hard-
ener" and "etch" and fastened to the press before it could be printed.
After printing, each master had to be removed from the press, and
the blanket wiped. After the printing was finished for the day the
press and environs had to be cleaned up. During actual printing
there were also delays. The cards might print too light or too
dark, or the like, and the press had to be stopped while the ink
supply was adjusted. Thus it would be seriously misleading to estimate the time actually required to perform any job solely on the
basis of the theoretical output of the machine during the time it is
actually running. If the press had been kept busy for a longer

period each day, and there had been fewer different masters to
handle, the relation of running time to total time would have been
more closely the same, but it will never be identical.

Writers, when referring to circulation systems, frequently
confuse a type of charging or stamping machine with the total system.   Individuals refer to Gaylord or Dickman Circulation Systems
when in reality these use the same basic system for discharging,
overdues, reserves, etc., and only the charging machines differ.
Likewise, it is not unusual to see a reference to one or another
photographic circulation system.   There are many devices on the
market but the basic system is the same -- i.e., numerical-time
control or transaction charging.   For several years, the preoccupation with machines led manufacturers to develop newer, faster machines, but in most libraries one-half second or one second saved
per book charged was not critical one way or another.   Once librarians began to adopt the systems study approach, the machine
was put into its proper perspective.

Gathering the Data

Although the particular data to be gathered will depend upon
the nature of the problem, the job studied and the availability of information, it is possible to identify several categories and to arrange these categories into a logical order.   First, it is necessary
to determine precisely of what steps (motion study) a job consists.
The next step is to determine the time required (time study) to perform each element.   Once the frequency of performance per unit of
work is learned, it is then possible to calculate the costs.   In addition to cost calculations, time data is essential in developing time
standards for work production.   Most of the remainder of this text
is devoted to descriptions of the useful data-gathering tools.

Analyzing the Present Method

After the analyst has identified and recorded each step of the
present method, the next job is to analyze the method.   To do this,
it is necessary to analyze each step of the process as well as the
process as a whole.   The following six questions will prove invalu-
able in analyzing a job:

1. Why? Why is the job done? Is it necessary? Many libraries maintain both alphabetical and numerical borrower registration files. Why are both needed? Why is one needed?

2. What? What is the purpose of the step in terms of the purposes of the library. What does it contribute to the overall process? The what and why can sometimes be combined into one question. For example, why are registration files maintained, and what are they used for?

3. Where? Where is the job performed? Where else could it be done? If work stations involving related jobs can be grouped together, time-consuming transportations can be lessened, or in some cases, even eliminated.

4. When? When should the job be done? Can it be performed at some different time to better advantage? Although book slipping can best be done during slack periods, some libraries attempt to keep abreast of returns even during rush hours.

5. Who? Who should do the job? Can it be done at less cost by a person with less training? This involves separating clerical and professional library duties.

6. How? How is the job done? How might it be done better?

Developing an Improved Method

There are several approaches to developing an improved method: 1) eliminate the routine as a whole or all unnecessary operations; 2) combine operations; 3) change the sequence in which operations are performed; 4) change the operator; and 5) simplify all remaining operations. When undertaking to develop a better method, the analyst should strive to remain free from constraints imposed by the present equipment, space or methods and to aim at an ideal solution. Later this solution can, if necessary, be modified to conform with reality.

Eliminating Unnecessary Operations

All too often, work is performed that need not be performed at all. The primary objective of management studies should be

elimination of unnecessary operations. Frequently one will encounter cries of anguish, predicting catastrophe if a particular operation is eliminated or a file discarded. One way to test the
feasibility of eliminating a step -- for instance accessioning, or
keeping an accession book -- is to stop doing it on an experimental
basis. If no serious problems develop within a reasonable, stated,
period of time, then eliminate the process permanently. It is not
necessary to throw away a file to see if it will be missed when it
gone. You are, for example, the head of a circulation department
and want to test the feasibility of eliminating a registration file of
one sort or another. Just move the file to your office, or give it
to your secretary if you have one, and mark clearly at its former
location where it is now located. You will soon know how and how
much the file is or is not used. On occasion there may be reper-
cussions after a file or operation has been eliminated. This, however, does not necessarily mean elimination was unjustified. The
total cost or overall efficiency, and not the cost or efficiency of any
one sub-step, must be the criterion. This question can also be approached in terms of risk: that is, what is the worst thing that
could happen, and what penalty would have to be paid? There are
many library examples to illustrate the question of cost vs. risk or
service vs. risk.

Searching shelves for overdue books prior to sending a notice is a time-consuming operation. If books are seldom found on
the shelf, then the operation should be eliminated. The worst that
can happen is for the library to send a notice to a patron who has
already returned his book. Friction arising from such situations
can be removed if the library adapts a business technique to its
ends by including on the overdue notice a sentence to the effect that
if the patron has already returned his book, to please disregard the
notice. This can eliminate an operation without noticeably affecting
service to the public.

Frequently the benefits accruing from a process are not justified by the costs of performing that process. For example, an acquisition department of a college library, as a routine matter,
checked all incoming books against their public catalog, to catch

any duplicates that were missed in the initial ordering so that they could be returned to the book dealer for a refund. Subsequent study showed clearly that, even though a duplicate was caught from time to time, more money, in the form of labor cost, was being consumed in the checking than was being saved on the refunds and the checking was discontinued.

Combining Operations and Files

Combining two or more operations into one will often produce dramatic savings. The potential in libraries for combining operations can be particularly rewarding because of the abundance of files and tasks involving multiple inspections. Order department records are sometimes divided into an outstanding order file, an in-process file, and an LC cards ordered file. (There are other possible variations.) These three files can be combined into one central file. As a result searching, filing, processing time is significantly reduced without losing essential information. Serial records for checking-in, paying, binding, and so forth also lend themselves readily to consolidation. This consolidation may be achieved in a very simple manner by the use of appropriate rubber stamps, signal tabs, multiple copies of the slip stapled together (each serving a different function) and so on.

Other everyday examples of combining operations are the now generally-accepted library practices of typing fanfolds (multiforms) for ordering books and for sending overdue notices. These forms have eliminated needless typing, inspections and movements.

Changing the Sequence of Operations

Rearranging the sequence in which a job is performed will often produce substantial savings. For example, a library which orders mostly new trade books will be able to obtain catalog cards for practically every title ordered. Nevertheless, some libraries defer ordering catalog cards until a title has been actually received because it does not wish to waste money on cards for books the library does not receive. However, ordering cards when the book is ordered will not only reduce time lag in processing but may also save the library money.

Changing the Operator

A job that can be performed by a person with less skill or training than the present operator should be reassigned to the former. This point is particularly pertinent in libraries in view of the constant efforts to distinguish between professional and non-professional work. In many libraries a cataloger is responsible for collecting and recording all information found on a unit catalog card. In other libraries the descriptive cataloging has been reassigned to non-professionals, often referred to as precatalogers. The question here is not which tasks are professional and which are not, but rather is one of improving utilization of professional librarians, who are in short supply.

Simplifying the Remaining Operations

Once a process has been analyzed and all worthwhile improvements are incorporated, the analyst can redirect his attention to the individual operations of the process and try to improve or simplify them. One method for accomplishing this is to employ the six questions that were used in analyzing the present method: why, what, when, who, where, and how?

Putting the Improved Method Into Operation

Presenting Plans to Supervisor

No suggestions for change will get very far unless the supervisor concerned is cooperative. Suggestions should be presented to him in writing. It should be remembered that unless this person has been deeply involved in the day-to-day progress of the study, he cannot be expected to grasp every detail instantly and easily. It is worth the effort to write up the proposal in a form appropriate for his, rather than your own, consumption. Abstract, emphasize, outline, omit irrelevant details -- make it easy for him to read and understand. Only after the supervisor has agreed to the proposals, or agreed to them with some additional suggestions (which might be good ones) can the new method be installed.

Overcoming Resistance

Gaining human acceptance for a new and improved work procedure is the single most critical task in introducing a new method. Human beings, with very few exceptions, tend to resist change. Although resistance may not always be encountered, the analyst should expect some difficulties. (The only certain exception to this rule might be a change involving only one person, and that person the same one who made the study.)

One basis of resistance is fear. The worker is afraid that an analysis of his job might reveal that he has been performing it inefficiently, and that this might lead to his dismissal on grounds of incompetence. It is a rare individual indeed who will deliberately perform his job inefficiently; but it is very common for an individual unknowingly to work inefficiently. There should be absolutely no reason for a worker to feel uneasy if he has been taught an inefficient method; the fault is usually that of the supervisor who gave him only meager instruction or no job instruction at all. The management analyst does strive to improve efficiency and thus increase production, but he is not trying to increase production at the expense of the worker.

The worker is sometimes afraid that a study will result in elimination of his job. Whenever a job is eliminated, the employee should be reassigned and retrained to perform more useful work and thus increase his contribution to the library. In this day of acute shortage of skilled workers it is incomprehensible that a competent person, even if his particular job were eliminated, should lack other employment in the same library system.

Another type of resistance frequently encountered is simple opposition to change. Change requires effort, and most humans by nature prefer the status quo. It is easier to continue in the accustomed manner. This is far from an unmitigated evil, for it insures a much more orderly and predictable society than could otherwise be the case. However, this natural resistance does increase the difficulty of carrying out scientific management studies and putting into effect the improvements arising from them. A third type of resistance arises from the fact that the worker is being studied. Even when he is able to grasp the logic and justice of the study and has no fear of the results from it, he may still not be happy about it.   People prefer to be at the eyepiece instead of the objective end of a microscope.

Although any person attempting to introduce a new work procedure cannot expect to change human nature, he can operate in such a manner as to keep resistance minimal.   The time to begin this process is at the beginning of the study.   An analyst cannot be too careful to inform all persons involved of the exact nature and purpose of the study.   It does not hurt to repeat this information many different times, to be sure that the message is communicated.

Staff participation should be encouraged as much as possible. For example, suppose that some sort of registration file was discontinued on an experimental basis, for a definite period of time. During the experiment staff members are invited to submit specific difficulties they have encountered.   In addition to encouraging staff participation, such a technique helps confine complaints to specific instances which in turn helps to keep the experiment as objective as possible.   It also helps some workers to understand the logic underlying the final decision.

Staff suggestions concerning the study itself should be encouraged.   Initially, most of the staff will remain reticent, but if the administration is sincere its receptive attitude will gradually be picked up by the staff and participation will mushroom.

Training Workers in the New Procedure

Assuming that workers have been kept informed of developments from the beginning of the study, and that any new equipment needed has been purchased or rented, training workers in the new procedure can begin.   It is very important that the supervisor be thoroughly trained in the new procedure.   A staff management man (and particularly an outside consultant) will very shortly turn his attention to new assignments in other departments or libraries.   Then it is the supervisor who must carry the major burden for installing the new procedure(s), and who must train employees to perform the new method.   Note that this training takes place before the new procedure is given its official test.   People are normally clumsy

at performing a new method until it becomes habitual, and if they
are not trained first, a new procedure may not receive a fair trial.

Initiating a Trial Operation and Following It Up

　　Do not expect too much initially and warn others not to.
Even with their preliminary training, depending on the length of
training the management man can persuade an administrator to provide and the complexity of the task, workers may still need some
time to become completely comfortable with the new procedure, and
attain a "job rhythm." It is easy for the management analyst or
supervisor, who always have many other problems awaiting their attention, to relax their vigilance too soon.   All too often expected
savings fail to materialize because a defective follow-up program
failed to detect some unexpected procedural difficulty or inadequately trained workers.   Experience has shown that an inadequately
trained worker is likely to become lax and revert to his former
method.   The length of follow-up should be based on the requirements of an individual situation, and not on some arbitrary period
of time.   It is certainly false economy to try to save a penny on
the final step at the risk of failure of an otherwise excellent routine.

Bibliography

General

Barnes, Ralph M.   Motion and Time Study.   5th ed.   New York:
　　Wiley, 1963.   Chapters 3-6.

Internal Revenue Service, Data Processing Systems Division.   Sys-
　　tems and Procedures: a Notebook for the Systems Man.
　　Washington, D. C. :   U. S. Government Printing Office, 1963.

Lehrer, Robert N.   Work Simplification.   Englewood Cliffs, N. J. ,
　　Prentice-Hall, 1957.

Mundel, Marvin E.   Motion and Time Study.   3rd ed.   Englewood
　　Cliffs, N. J. ,   Prentice-Hall, 1960.   Chapters 1-4.

Zinck, W. Clements.   Dynamic Work Simplification.   New York:
　　Reinhold, 1962.

Libraries

Blasingame, Ralph U.   'Work Simplification in Libraries," News
　　Notes of California Libraries.   XLVIII, No. 2 (April, 1953).
　　p. 328-33.

Corbett, Edmund V.   Public Library Finance and Accountancy.
      London: The Library Association, 1960.   Chapter 9, "Cost
      Accounting: Organisation and Methods."

Kingery, Robert E.   'What Happens When the Management Engi-
      neers Leave?" College and Research Libraries, XV, No. 2
      (April, 1954), p. 202-04.

Morris, T. D.   "The Management Consultant in the Library,"
      College and Research Libraries, XV, No. 2 (April, 1954),
      p. 196-201.

Rogers, Frank B.   "Management Improvement in the Library,"
      Bulletin of the Medical Library Association, XLVIII, No. 3
      (July, 1957), p. 404-09.

Shaw, Ralph R.   'Documentation: Complete Cycle of Information
      Service," College and Research Libraries, XVIII, No. 6
      (November, 1957), p. 452-54.

Tauber, Maurice F.   "Management Improvements in Libraries,"
      College and Research Libraries, XV, No. 2 (April, 1954),
      p. 188-96.

Woodruff, Elaine.   'Work Measurement Applied to Libraries,"
      Special Libraries, XLVIII, No. 4 (April, 1957), p. 139-44.

Chapter III
The Flow Process Chart, Flow Diagram
and Block Diagram

In management work it is always necessary to analyze operations in step-by-step detail. Several fairly standard charting procedures have been developed to aid in this analysis. In this chapter, attention will be concentrated on the flow process chart. There are also other process charts designed for special uses. For example, the man-machine chart is used for studying processes involving an interplay between man and machine, and the gang process chart is used for studying the actions of a group of workers laboring as a unit, such as a truck-loading crew. Although these special charts can be applied to certain library situations, they are, by and large, less useful to librarians than the versatile flow process chart.

Block Diagram

A crucial step of any management study, necessary regardless of the type of job involved, is to identify and define the scope of the study. Too often this initial overview is forgotten or neglected. The result can often be that the analyst will wind up with data that is biased. For example, we have heard for a long time about the fantastic speed of computers. What we are not always aware of are the time and effort it may take before the computer is turned on to operate according to a program and to convert intelligible language into machine readable language. If a study does not take cognizance of preparation time, its conclusion must be suspect.

A block diagram provides an investigator with this important initial overview. It is a graphic representation of a series of operations, processes or sub-processes that collectively comprise a system. Constructing a block diagram is not difficult. Try to visualize the system in its entirety. Then ask such questions as:

Are there other processes which are influenced by or have an influence on the system about to be studied? If so, how are they related? What is the direction of the work flows?

Figure 3-1 represents a block diagram for a typical circulation system. When one refers to a circulation system, the routines that one usually thinks of first are the charging and discharging procedures. The relevance or even pertinence of some of the other routines might not at first glance be apparent. For instance, the book preparation procedures (putting on of plastic jackets, typing of book cards, pasting on book pockets, etc.) are frequently considered to be a part of technical processing, but in some libraries these operations are performed solely for the purpose of preparing the book for circulation. One way to make this distinction is to compare what would be done to the same book if it were not going to be circulated.

One difficulty which occasionally occurs in preparing a block diagram is that it isn't always possible to show exact relationships or directions of work flows between processes. To illustrate, where does a renewal procedure fit in (See Figure 3-1)? In some systems, renewals are made in person or by telephone or both; in others, the book is simply discharged and re-charged. And some libraries have eliminated the question of renewals by an administrative edict. But these problems, if encountered, are not serious. As long as the relevant relationships are considered during the initial planning stages, the diagram has served its purpose.

Figure 3-2 is an example of a more complex block diagram, illustrating one procedure for book screening, and pre-cataloging. However, despite the additional complexity, the principles of diagramming are exactly the same as for Figure 3-1.

Flow Diagram

A flow diagram is a graphic view of a work area upon which is superimposed the path or movement of workers or the flow of materials. It can be used in conjunction with a flow process study or separately. The flow diagram is an excellent tool for jobs that require considerable movement of either persons or products.

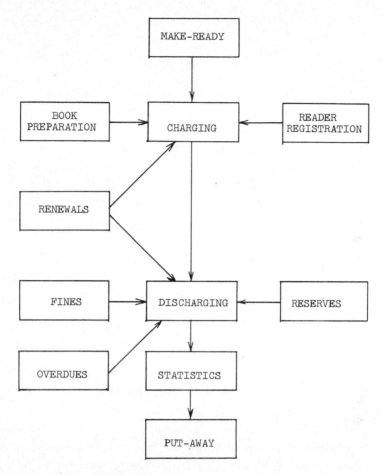

Fig. 3-1 Block diagram of a circulation system

Everyone knows that "one picture is worth a thousand words." For
example, a library reference department had its ready reference
collection located in an area thirty feet from its reference desk.
No one really knew why the books had been placed there originally.
Although there was an occasional complaint because the collection
was not convenient, the walk really didn't seem to bother anyone.
One of the assistants drew a diagram of the area and kept track of
the number of trips to and from this stack area made during one

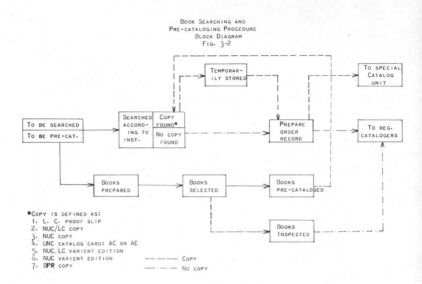

Book Searching and
Pre-cataloging Procedure
Block Diagram
Fig. 3-2

*Copy is defined as:
1. L. C. proof slip
2. NUC/LC copy
3. NUC copy
4. UNC catalog card: AC or AE
5. NUC/LC varient edition
6. NUC varient edition
7. BPR copy

— — — Copy
— · — No copy

afternoon.   He found that during the period observed thirty-five
round trips were made and that the average distance traveled per
trip was 95 feet.   Thus the reference staff had walked over a half
mile to locate books in one afternoon.   In view of his experiment
the assistant suggested that the ready reference collection be relocated behind the reference desk.   This change would eliminate over
ninety per cent of the walking (See Figure 3-3).   It was not many
days until his suggestion was adopted.

     Flow diagrams can be particularly useful in planning a new
building or remodeling an old one.   Traffic flows of both patrons
and library employees can be charted.   Undesirable flows can hopefully be either eliminated or minimized before the first brick is
laid.

     A floor plan makes an excellent diagram if one is available.

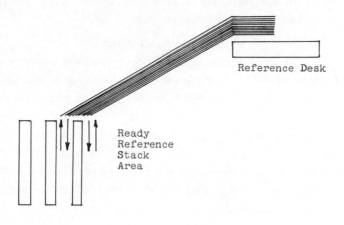

Reference Desk

Ready
Reference
Stack
Area

Original Arrangement

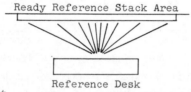

Ready Reference Stack Area

Reference Desk

New Arrangement

Fig. 3-3 Flow diagram depicting traffic flows created
by two alternate locations of a ready reference collection.

For most library studies, however, architectural precision is not
required; a home-made diagram will prove equally satisfactory.
First, sketch in all furniture and equipment. Although the furniture does not need to be drawn to scale, some pains should be
taken to maintain the general proportions. The route taken by the
person or product as he or it proceeds from work station to work
station should be represented by a line. Distances travelled should
be paced rather than estimated. As an experiment, chart the route
a new book takes from the time it enters the library until it is
placed on a shelf ready for use. On the diagram, plot the book's
course as it progresses through the processing areas. Note what

operations are performed at each work station. This exercise can
sometimes be a revealing experience.

Flow Process Chart

The flow process chart is one of the most versatile and useful tools available for analyzing library jobs. It is a graphic
means of portraying the work involved in a job where the person
or product (form) charted moves from work station to work station.
The chart also includes the distance traveled and the amount of
time required to perform each operation. The flow process chart
can be used to record either the activities of a person or the operations performed on a product. However, both should not be
charted simultaneously. If it should become necessary to chart
both, separate charts should be prepared.

Flow Process Chart Symbols

The Gilbreths (see Chapter I) devised forty symbols to be
used in making process charts, but this number has been gradually
reduced. In 1947, the American Society of Mechanical Engineers
established a set of five standard symbols. During the intervening
years, more and more industries have adopted these ASME symbols. They will be used in this text. The five symbols used in
flow process charting are defined and illustrated in Figure 3-4.
While there is no hard and fast rule against using other symbols,
it is wise to retain a set once people have become accustomed to
it. There might occasionally be a situation that calls for a new
symbol. This might occur, for instance, in charting a job that involves a considerable number of operations that are unproductive --
that is, that do not contribute to the completion of the process. In
such a situation, it might be useful to differentiate between the productive and non-productive operations by using two different symbols. Decisions of this nature will depend upon the job in question.

Constructing a Flow Process Chart

A flow process chart can be made on any number of forms.
As long as provisions are made for including certain categories of
information, even blank paper is satisfactory. Figure 3-5 is an
example of a typical flow process chart of a library routine.

Symbol	Name	Symbol Representation
○	Operation	An action which usually results in a modification of the product studied, or an action performed by a person which contributes to the completion of a process. (Examples: stamping the date on a book card, opening a carton of books.)
⇨	Transportation	A change in location of a person or product from one place to another unless movement is an integral part of the operation or an inspection. (Examples: books trucked from a circulation desk to a stack area, a mail clerk moving from office to office distributing mail.)
▽	Storage	A permanent storage or delay; a permanent storage is considered as any of an indefinite duration; also used to denote a controlled storage that requires an authorization for its removal. (Example: cards filed in a card catalog.)
◗	Delay	Delay that is not permanent; something that temporarily holds up the immediate performance of the next step in a process. (Examples: waiting for an elevator, a letter in an out basket.)
□	Inspection	Quality or quantity inspection made against a predetermined standard. (Examples: no. of cards to be filed during a given time interval (quantity); no. and types of errors that will be tolerated on a catalog card (quality).
⊡	Combined Symbols	Activities performed at the same work place or at the same time as one activity. (Example: a combined operation-inspection.)

Fig. 3-4   Process chart symbols

_____

[a] Operation and Flow Process Charts, ASME Standard 101, published by the American Society of Mechanical Engineers, New York, 1947.

The Heading of the form should include: 1) who or what is charted;   2) whether the chart represents the present or proposed

method;   3) the starting and finishing point of the chart;   4) the
name of the analyst;   5) the date that the process is charted, and
6) a tabular summary block for comparing the present and proposed
methods.   As an example, see the heading of Figure 3-5.

First of all, decide what or who is to be charted.   Will the
study require observing what a person does or what is done to a
product or form?   Once decided, the subject should not be changed.
One way to prevent inadvertent switching is to fill out the form in
the active voice if a person is being observed, and in the passive
voice when operations are performed on a product.

Choose a definite starting and finishing point.   Be sure no
part of the process or system is omitted.   A block diagram will
prove useful at this point.   Don't forget to include all make-ready
(preparatory) and put-away (clean-up) operations.

Chart each step in the process even though it might appear
to be unimportant or superfluous.   It's much better to include too
much detail than not enough.   An operation that has not been
charted cannot be eliminated.   The job should be charted as it is
actually performed and not as one thinks it should be performed.
This error is easy to make when one is simultaneously observing
and thinking of possible improvements and suddenly realizes that a
particular step or series of steps are useless.   But it should be
re-emphasized that the first step is to complete the chart for the
job as it is performed, and only then to concentrate on improvements.   It is usually wise to make a few trial runs.   This enables
the analyst to familiarize himself with the process and to observe
and learn which operations are performed during each job cycle.
A trial period also provides the worker with an opportunity to shed
his initial nervousness and to become accustomed to the presence
of the analyst.

Once the charting is finished, calculate the number of operations performed, the number of transportations observed, the distances travelled, the number of delays, etc.   These figures are recorded in the summary block.

Normally, the analyst will finish with two sets of charts for
each process charted: one for the present method and one for the

FLOW PROCESS CHART	SUMMARY		

Subject Charted: <u>Mrs. Jones: Preparation of books for circulation.</u>

Present [x] or Proposed [ ] Method   Type of Chart [x] Man [ ] Product

Chart Begins: <u>Walks to closet.</u>

Chart Ends: <u>Returns to desk.</u>

Charted By: R. Smith   Date: <u>9/12/66</u>   Sheet <u>1</u> of <u>1</u>

	Pres. Meth.	Prop. Meth.	Diff.
Operations	20		
Transportations	4		
Inspections	1		
Delays			
Distance in feet	60		

Dist. in feet	Time in Min.	Symbol	Step no.	Description of Event
15			1.	Walks to closet.
			2.	Picks up book slips, book pockets, and glue.
15			3.	Returns to desk.
			4.	Places book slips, book pockets, and glue on table adjacent to desk.
			5.	Sits down.
			6.	Uncovers typewriter.
			7.	Reaches for first book on book truck.
			8.	Opens book.
			9.	Removes order card from book.
			10.	Discards order slip.
			11.	Inspects for reference book.
				NOTE: No preparation for reference books.
			12.	Inserts book pocket and book slip into typewriter.
			13.	Types book information and date onto both cards.
			14.	Removes cards from machine.
			15.	Stamps accession number on book slip.
			16.	Stamps accession number on book pocket.
			17.	Stamps accession number on verso of title page.
			18.	Glues pocket into book.
			19.	Closes book.
			20.	Places book on book truck.
			21.	Covers typewriter.
			22.	Picks up book slips, book pockets, and glue.
15			23.	Walks to closet.
			24.	Puts away materials.
15			25.	Returns to desk.

Fig. 3-5 Example of a typical flow process chart of a library routine.

proposed method.   If the analyst is working in a situation where he
is acting both as the staff officer and the line officer, he will use
the information he has gathered to develop and implement a new
job method.   On the other hand, if the staff and line officers are
different individuals, the analyst will report his findings and recommendations to the proper authority.

One of the easiest ways to learn how to chart is to begin
with something familiar.   For example, shaving in the morning,
mixing cocktails, setting the dinner table, etc.   Most problems
which one can expect to encounter on the job will be encountered in
charting these familiar daily routines.

Charting Sub-Procedures

Most jobs associated with the machine tool industry, and,
for that matter, most jobs in assembly plants are highly repetitious; that is, the job is done the same way each time.   This is
not always the case in library situations.   Occasionally, it is necessary to make allowances for decisions that alter the usual procedure.   For lack of a better term, these can be described as
"sub-procedures."

This problem and its solution can be illustrated by the reserve procedures of a numerical-time control circulation system
(transaction charging).   In many cases a book requested will already be on reserve.   If it is not already on reserve and is owned
by the library, a second procedure must be followed.   If the book
is not owned by the library, but is already on order, still a third
procedure is necessary.   Finally, if the book is neither owned by
the library nor on order, a fourth procedure is required.   It is
necessary to identify and clearly distinguish all of these sub-procedures if one is to arrive at an accurate systems cost.   This is
true because each of these sub-procedures will have a different frequency of occurrence.   For example, a library might receive a total of 2,000 reserve requests during one year, of which 1,000 are
for titles already on reserve, 500 for titles owned by the library
but not on reserve, 300 for books already on order, and the remaining 200 for titles neither owned nor on order.   In order to cal-

culate a total cost, the cost of each sub-procedure will have to be calculated.   A flow process chart of an entire reserve process may be found in Chapter XII.

Analyzing the Present Method and
Developing and Improved Method

One of the most challenging and interesting aspects of method analysis is developing a new and improved method.   There are few concrete guides; much depends on the acumen and ingenuity of the analyst.   There are, of course, the six basic questions: why, what, when, where, who, and how.   Each step of the present process should be questioned, even when the step appears to be absolutely indispensable.   A new method can be developed by eliminating steps, combining steps, rearranging the sequence of steps, changing the operator, etc. (See Chapter II).

Let us now consider a specific example.   It is increasingly common for city, county, and regional library systems to apply centralized ordering and processing procedures.   Books are not received by the branches until they are ready for use.   Once the books arrive at a branch, they must be unpacked.   Figure 3-6 is a flow process chart describing this process as it actually took place at one branch.

Before proceeding with the questioning of each step in Figure 3-6, it will be worthwhile to direct some attention to the process as a whole.   Why perform the job at all?   All would probably agree that it is necessary to unpack new books, and that some preparation is necessary before the books can be displayed to the public.   The problem is to ascertain how much is necessary.

When is the job being performed?   This would certainly be pertinent if it were found that the job was being performed during rush hours, particularly during the hours immediately after school lets out.

Who performs the job?   In this case, the branch librarian. One can question the need for a professional librarian to unpack books.   It would appear to be a more appropriate task for a sub-professional, or even better, a student assistant.   One objection voiced in such situations is that if the librarian doesn't perform

FLOW PROCESS CHART

			SUMMARY		
			Pres. Meth.	Prop. Meth.	Diff.
Subject Charted: Branch librarian unpacking a shipment of new books.					
Present [X] or Proposed [ ] Method Type of Chart [X] Man [ ] Product	Operations				
Chart Begins: Transports book truck to unloading area.	Transportations				
Chart Ends: Transports books to next work station.	Inspections				
Charted By: J. Smith Date: 11/17/66 Sheet 1 of 2	Delays				
	Distance in feet				

Dist. in feet	Time in Min.	Symbol	Step no.	Description of Event
25			1.	Transports book truck to unloading area.
			2.	Opens first box.
			3.	Takes first book from box.
			4.	Opens back cover.
			5.	Locates book pocket.
			6.	Inspects book card (in book pocket) and book pocket to ensure that an accession number has been stamped.
			7.	Pulls set of catalog cards from book pocket.
			8.	Sets catalog cards aside for filing later.
			9.	Inspects color of book card: different colors used to distinguish adult from children's books.
4			10.	Walks to outstanding order file.
			11.	Pulls branch's copy of original order request from file.
			12.	Discards this copy.
			13.	Picks up embossing stamp.
			14.	Opens book to page nineteen.
			15.	Stamps ownership mark on page nineteen.
			16.	Closes book.
			17.	Places book on book truck.
			18.	Returns to box of books.
				NOTE: Steps two through eighteen are repeated until all books are unloaded and checked-in. (See "re-cycle" arrow).
			19.	Opens desk drawer.
			20.	Takes out statistics book.

Fig. 3-6 Flow process chart of the process of unpacking a shipment of new books at a branch library.

FLOW PROCESS CHART					SUMMARY			
						Pres. Meth.	Prop. Meth.	Diff.
Subject Charted: Branch librarian unpacking a shipment of new books.					Operations	22		
Present [X] or Proposed [ ] Method Type of Chart [X] Man [ ] Product					Transportations	3		
Chart Begins: Transports book truck to unloading area.					Inspections	2		
Chart Ends: Transports books to next work station.					Delays			
Charted By: J. Smith Date: 11/17/66 Sheet 2 of 2					Distance in feet	49		

Dist. in feet	Time in Min.	Symbol	Step no.	Description of Event
		○	21.	Counts new adult books. NOTE: These have been placed on a separate shelf.
		○	22.	Enters count in statistics book.
		○	23.	Counts juvenile titles.
		○	24.	Enters count into statistics book.
		○	25.	Returns statistics book to drawer.
		○	26.	Closes drawer.
20		⇨	27.	Transports books to next work station.

Fig. 3-6 (Continued)

these tasks, there will be no opportunity for him to familiarize himself with new titles. Obviously, the question is not whether the librarian should or should not examine new receipts, but rather, when. There may be more suitable times than during the unloading process. So our examination of the job as a totality has caused us to decide that the job should be performed by a less-skilled worker.

Having completed the overall examination, the questioning of each step now begins. In Step 1, for instance, why is it necessary for the branch staff member to transport the new books into the processing area? Wouldn't it be more efficient if the delivery attendant delivered the boxes directly to the point where they will be unpacked? From Step 2 through Step 18, there are numerous questions that might be asked. Why not empty all of the books onto book trucks instead of one at a time? Why bother inspecting to see

if the book has been accessioned? We have every reason to assume it has been, and if, once in a great, great while one isn't,
it can hardly cause any significant harm. Why inspect the color of
each book card? The answer is to separate the juvenile and adult
books; but since they were processed separately at central processing, just keeping them separate there and then shipping to the
branch in separate containers would eliminate the need to inspect
the cards. If the catalog cards are sent in a separate packet along
with a copy of the original order card, then all need for the branch
unpacker to open the book pocket would be eliminated. Why clear
the outstanding order file piecemeal? If the copies of the original
order card come in a separate packet, it will prove more convenient to clear the orders in a batch. Batching will eliminate many
trips to the outstanding orders file. Since central processing is
provided, why not stamp the "secret page" there, where it could be
done on a faster, mass-production basis?

Some even more fundamental questions could be asked. For
example, what indispensable purpose does accessioning serve?
Would there really be any serious consequences if it were done
away with entirely? With regard to the secret page, why bother to
stamp it in the first place? How many lost or stolen books have
actually been recovered with its aid? Is it always necessary for a
branch library to maintain an order file, which is a complete duplication of the central file? It might be possible to eliminate such
files by installing an intra-system communications system. In our
example, these decisions are beyond the authority of the branch library personnel. However, if the central processing administrator
posed the same questions, these procedures might well be changed.

Figure 3-7 shows the improved unpacking and preparation
process. Note that the work is now performed by a sub-professional, who later delivers the processed books to the branch librarian
for his examination. Examination of the summary box in Figure
3-7 reveals that the number of steps has been reduced from 27 to
11.

For a much more comprehensive example of flow process
charting present and proposed methods, see Chapters XII and XIII.

				FLOW PROCESS CHART		SUMMARY			

FLOW PROCESS CHART

			SUMMARY		
			Pres. Meth.	Prop. Meth.	Diff.
Subject Charted: Branch sub-professional unpacking a shipment of new books.					
		Operations			
Present ☐ or Proposed ☒ Method Type of Chart ☒ Man ☐ Product					
		Transportations			
Chart Begins: Opens first box of books.					
		Inspections			
Chart Ends: Transports truck of new books to desk of librarian.					
		Delays			
Charted By: J. Smith Date: 11/19/66 Sheet 1 of 2					
		Distance in feet			

Dist. in feet	Time in Min.	Symbol	Step no.	Description of Event
		○	1.	Opens first box of books. NOTE: Delivery truck personnel have previously piled boxes of books in processing area.
		○	2.	Picks up batch of books from box. NOTE: Work is being batched instead of being handled in sequence cycle by cycle.
		○	3.	Places adult books on one book truck; juvenile titles are placed on a second truck. NOTE: Juvenile and adult titles are processed separately at the main library, and shipped to the branch in separate containers. NOTE: Steps one through three are repeated until all books are placed on book trucks.
		○	4.	Takes statistics book from shelf.
		○	5.	Counts adult volumes.
		○	6.	Enters count into statistics book.
		○	7.	Counts juvenile volumes.
		○	8.	Enters count into statistics book. NOTE: The book card and pocket are no longer inspected to make certain the accession number has been stamped on them.
		○	9.	Returns statistics book to shelf. NOTE: Branch personnel no longer reinspect work of central agency. Secret page is not embossed. Catalog cards are sent separately along with a copy of the original order card.

Fig. 3-7 Flow process chart of the process
of unpacking a shipment of new books
at a branch library.

FLOW PROCESS CHART

			SUMMARY			
Subject Charted: <u>Branch sub-professional unpacking a</u> <u>shipment of new books.</u>				Pres. Meth.	Prop. Meth.	Diff.
			Operations	22	10	12
Present ☐ or Proposed ☒ Method Type of Chart ☒ Man ☐ Product			Transpor- tations	3	1	2
Chart Begins: <u>Opens first box of books.</u>			Inspections	2	--	2
Chart Ends: <u>Transports truck of new books to desk of</u> <u>librarian.</u>			Delays			
Charted By: J. Smith Date: 11/23/66 Sheet 2 of 2			Distance in feet	49	30	19

Dist. in feet	Time in Min.	Symbol	Step no.	Description of Event
		○	10.	Clears outstanding order file.
				NOTE: A clerk will either clear the branch's copies of the original order requests all in a batch now or later during a slack work period.
30		⇨	11.	Transports truck to librarian's desk.
				NOTE: This is not a work inspection, but an opportunity for the branch librarian to familiarize himself with new titles in a more comfortable and efficient manner than would be possible while distracted by the details of the unpacking process.

Fig. 3-7   (Continued)

Use of Check-Lists

One approach to the problem of improving job methods is to subject the process to a series of specific and detailed questions. Lists have been developed for all phases of a methods study, including materials handling, use of machines, studying the operator, and the workers' environment.   One such list is shown below. However, it should be remembered that no list will ever supplant the curiosity of the imaginative analyst.

Sample Operation Check List

1. Can any steps be eliminated?
2. Can any steps be sub-divided?
3. Can any of the operations be combined?
4. Can the sequence of steps be altered?
5. Can part of the operation be performed more effectively

as a separate operation?

6. Could a lower paid employee do the operation?

7. Can another person do the job better?

8. Are work loads balanced?

9. Can peak loads of activity be eliminated?

10. Can delays be eliminated or utilized for other operations?

11. Can "bottleneck" operations be eliminated, rescheduled, etc. ?

12. Can the operation be done in another department to save time?

13. If the operation is changed, what effect will it have on other operations in the system?

14. Can spot checks (or inspections based on sampling techniques) be employed instead of 100 per cent inspections.

15. Is work being duplicated or performed in more than one location?

16. Can the faculty member, reader, or vendor be consulted to make both our and their operations easier and more economical?

Bibliography

American Society of Mechanical Engineers. Operations and Flow Process Charts. New York: American Society of Mechanical Engineers, 1947. (ASME Standard 101).

Barnes, Ralph M. Motion and Time Study. 5th ed. New York: Wiley, 1963. Chapter 7, "Process Analysis."

Maynard, Harold B., ed. Industrial Engineering Handbook. 2nd ed. New York: McGraw-Hill, 1963. Section 2, Chapter 3, "Process Chart Procedure."

Maynard, Harold B., and Stegemerten, G. J. Operations Analysis. New York: McGraw-Hill, 1939. Chapter 8, "Flow Process Charts."

Mundel, Marvin E. Motion and Time Study. 3rd ed. Englewood Cliffs, N. J., Prentice-Hall, 1960. Chapter 5, "Process Chart-Product Analysis;" Chapter 6, "Process Chart-Man Analysis."

Chapter IV
Decision Flow Charting

The development of computers necessitated new techniques for analyzing work. The computer is capable of performing operations such as addition, multiplication, subtraction, division, storage, shifting, and transfer of numbers through yes or no operations only. In order to employ it, work must be analyzed element by element, or decision by decision. The decision flow chart has been developed to aid in preparing detailed instructions for use in a computer. Flow charting, as this is termed in computer literature, is one of the preliminary steps in preparing a program for use in a computer. A decision flow chart can be defined as a graphic means of representing work flows which include the yes-no decisions and actions required to perform a designated task or series of tasks. Figures 4-3 and 4-4 are examples of such charts.

Library Applications

Library routines can be expressed in "yes" and "no" decisions. Whenever a book is discharged, the desk attendant checks to see if it is overdue. If the book is overdue (yes) the fine collection sub-routine is initiated; if not (no) the discharging routine is continued. If a fine is to be collected (yes) the attendant must initiate the collection sub-routine; if not (no) the basic routine continues; etc.

The Decision Flow Chart and the Flow Process Chart

The decision flow chart will find its greatest application in analyzing complicated work flows which require numerous decisions. The flow process chart, on the other hand, is best used for describing work when the operator simply adheres to a prescribed routine for each cycle. For example, machining the ends of casings on a turret lathe does not involve decisions once the basic procedure has been developed. However, once even a complicated sys-

52

tem with all of its sub-routines has been decision flow diagrammed, the flow process chart can then be employed to analyze each of the sub-routines.

Rules for Constructing a Decision Flow Chart

An analyst must be familiar with the work to be charted so that the job may be reduced to step-by-step instructions. Moreover, he must be familiar enough with the job to avoid the error of charting work as it might be performed rather than as it actually is performed. Aside from reducing a procedure to its elemental steps, there are only a few rules to be observed.

Each chart must have a logical starting and stopping point. The flows must reach a logical stopping point where no additional action is necessary.

All questions must be answerable by either "yes" or "no." If this is not possible, the original question must be rephrased. The questions should then be arranged so that the event most likely to occur first is asked first, the second questions next, and so on. This procedure is continued until all alternatives are exhausted.

The main flow (the trunk) consists of the decisions and actions that occur normally in a procedure. The alternative decisions and actions (the branch flows) represent the exceptions to the norm. For example, in Figure 4-3, when the ignition key is turned on, the normal reaction is for the motor to start. Therefore, the "yes" response "Motor start?" is located along the main trunk. However, since non-starting does occur occasionally, this alternative is represented to the side of the main trunk by an additional series of questions and actions.

Verbal descriptions must be brief but lucid; otherwise, the reader will find it difficult to follow the flow. Most library employees are not yet accustomed to reading and thinking in terms of various shaped boxes hung together by a network of arrows. Clearly written instructions will prove particularly helpful during the period of adjustment.

Mechanics of Constructing a Flow Decision Chart

Various shaped boxes which enclose the verbal descriptions are used to represent different types of instructions. The shape of the box is purely arbitrary, and there is no standard set of symbols. The primary reason for using different shaped boxes is to make it easier for the reader to distinguish between different types of instructions. The symbols used in this text with the explanations for their use are shown in Figure 4-1. An illustration of a diagramming template containing these symbols is shown in Figure 4-2.

Construction of a decision flow chart is often not as intellectually difficult as it is physically cumbersome. Most charts require tens of steps which necessitate using a large poster board or several pieces of paper. Different individuals have developed their own techniques. One method is to use poster board ranging from 3 ft. x 4 ft. to 4 ft. x 6 ft. in size, penciling in every step from beginning to end. Another method is to prepare a sheet of paper for each step. The sheets are then mounted on the board to show the total work flow.

Once the preliminary chart is constructed it should be examined closely for errors. It is usually wise to have two or more individuals check the chart. It is easy to omit a step, or what might turn out to be a whole series of steps. Once all corrections and modifications have been made, the chart can be redrawn for the procedure manual.

A decision flow chart can be constructed in one of two formats. The main flow can proceed from top to bottom of each page (See Figure 4-4), or from left to right (See Figure 4-3). With the former the branch flows are drawn to the left and right; and with the latter, above and below the main flow. Whenever possible all branches emanating from a "yes" alternative should be drawn on the same side of the main flow and those from a "no" alternative on the other side. Adherence to this convention produces a chart that is easier to read and interpret.

Symbols	Name	Explanation
	Question Box	The question must always be answerable with a "yes" or "no". If there are more than two choices, additional questions must be asked.
	Action Box	Any action taken. This is similar to an operation in a flow process chart. The size of the box depends solely on the amount of written description required to facilitate clarity.
	In Box	This symbol indicates a flow coming in from another chart, or from another part of the same chart.
	Out Box	The opposite of an in box. The point at which the flow line will be continued is written in the box.
	Hold Box	Material is received, held for a stated period, and then is released. If it goes in and comes out at the same point in the flow a double-ended arrow is used; if it goes in at one point and comes out at another, two arrows are used.
	Start or Stop	Beginning or end of a procedure.
	Explanation	For explanations but has no significance to the system itself.
Y	Yes Line	Leads from a question box to the box which answers "yes."
N	No Line	Leads from a question box to the box which answers "no."

Fig. 4-1   Flow decision chart symbols.[a]

---

[a] Louis Schultheiss, Don S. Culbertson, and Edward M. Heilinger. Advanced Data Processing in the University Library. (New York: Scarecrow Press, 1962) pp. 82-84. [The symbols used in the text were developed by IBM and subsequently adopted for use by the University of Illinois at Chicago Library.]

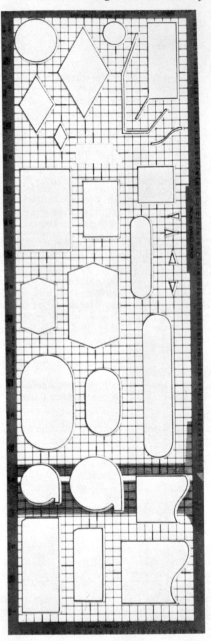

Figure 4-2

Practice is the surest way of learning how to prepare decision flow charts. A good way to begin is to chart familiar daily routines such as shaving, setting a table, shining shoes, or mixing cocktails. One such routine -- starting an automobile -- is shown in Figure 4-3.

A more complicated illustration relating to library work is shown in Figure 4-4. This chart was developed to aid a bibliographic staff in learning the processes of screening and searching when a book was physically available as contrasted to screening and searching when only an order card was available. The chart also provided the library with an effective training device for new searchers. In addition, it revealed that certain steps were unnecessary and these were eliminated.

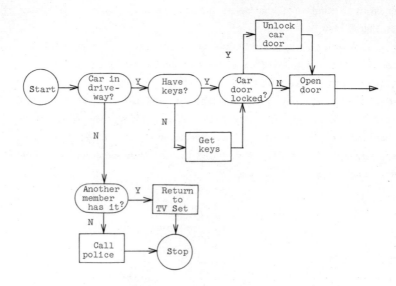

Fig. 4-3 Sample flow decision chart:
Starting an automobile.

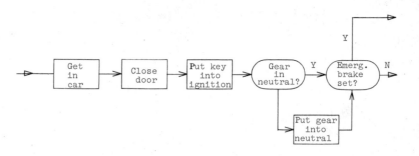

Fig. 4-3 (Continued)

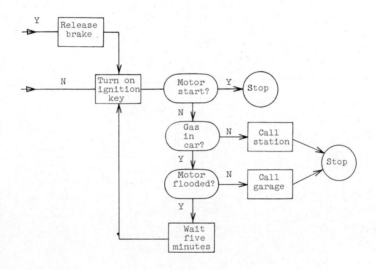

Fig. 4-3 (Continued)

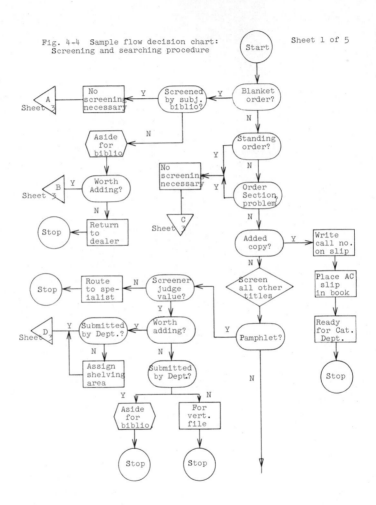

Fig. 4-4 Sample flow decision chart:
Screening and searching procedure

Sheet 1 of 5

Fig. 4-4 (Continued)

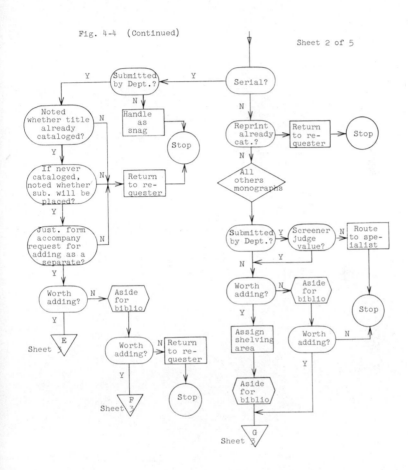

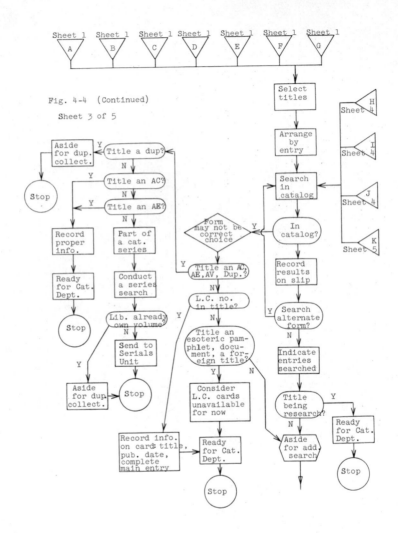

Fig. 4-4 (Continued)

Sheet 3 of 5

Fig. 4-4 (Continued)   Sheet 4 of 5

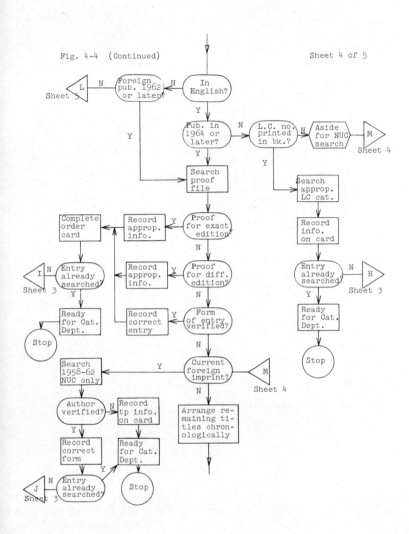

Fig. 4-4 (Continued)   Sheet 5 of 5

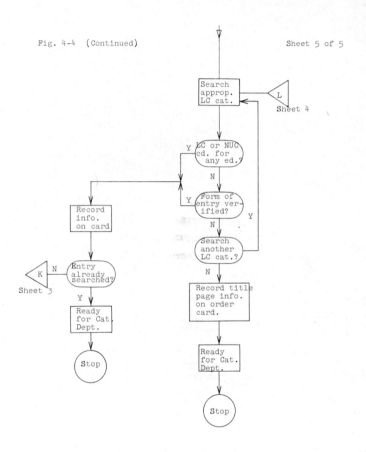

Bibliography

Goldhor, Herbert, ed. Proceedings of the 1963 Clinic on Library
     Applications of Data Processing, Held at the... Urbana
     Campus of the University of Illinois, April 28-May 1, 1963.
     Champaign, Ill., Distributed by the Illini Union Bookstore,
     1964.

     Article by Schultheiss, "Techniques of Flow-Charting,"
     p. 62-78.

Schultheiss, Louis A., Culbertson, Don S., and Heilinger, Edward
     M. Advanced Data Processing in the University Library.
     New York: Scarecrow Press, 1962.

Chapter V
Operations Analysis Including Some Principles
of Motion Economy

The flow process and decision flow charts will suffice for most studies. However, these tools are designed only to chart either a worker or a product as he or it moves from one work-place to another. As libraries grow in size and as the frequency with which routines are performed increases, the potential gains from analyzing work performed in one place will increase. Instead of studying gross body movements, a study will focus on the motions of the hands, or, possibly, the feet or eyes. This type of analysis can be performed with the aid of an operations chart, also known as a left-hand -- right-hand chart. This tool has not yet achieved widespread use in libraries. Its application is justified only when job frequency is high. However, such everyday library jobs as charging out books, discharging books, mending, labeling, typing catalog cards, and separating multiple forms are all suitable to operations charting. Operation analysis also focuses attention on the arrangement of the work area itself. Finally, operations study provides an opportunity to train workers in some of the basic principles of motion economy. Although these principles were developed for use in industry, they apply equally well to library-oriented tasks when the frequency with which a repetitive operation is performed is very high.

Making an Operations Chart

First, prepare a diagram of the work area. The diagram should show the arrangement of the work area, including all equipment and materials used in the performance of the job. Figure 5-1 shows such a diagram for a typical public library charging system. A flow diagram is usually not prepared to show hand movements. If hand motions were plotted, the resulting chart would be so littered with lines that it would become a meaningless maze.

66

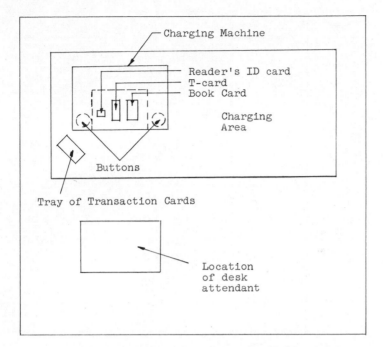

Fig. 5-1 Work area for a typical
public library charging system.

Instead, the diagram indicates the layout of the workplace.

The symbols used in operations analysis are almost identical with those used with the flow process chart. However, in the
operations chart, the symbol applies to a body member instead of
the entire body. These symbols are listed in Figure 5-2.

Select a logical beginning point, and observe several cycles
as a trial. Next, proceed to chart the movements of one hand
from beginning to end of the cycle. Although it would be more convenient for the analyst to observe and chart both hands together,
this, in practice, is usually too difficult. Once the process has
been charted for one hand, the entire process is charted for the
second hand. When both hands have been charted, it is necessary
to make sure that the activities performed simultaneously are lined
up horizontally on the chart. In order to insure this, it is usually

Symbol	Name	Explanation
◯	Operation	The body member (hand) does something, except when the hand is moving toward or from an object, or holding an object. (Examples: picking up, putting together, taking apart, or writing).
▷	Transportation	The body member (hand) moves toward an object or changes its location.
▽	Hold	The body member (hand) maintains an object in a fixed position so that work can be performed with it or upon it.
D	Delay	The body member (hand) is idle or is moving, but without purpose.

Fig. 5-2 Operation analysis symbols.

best to observe several additional cycles. Occasionally, one hand will perform several different activities while the other hand maintains a single one. In such cases the description for one hand will have to be repeated for two or more steps in succession. Figure 5-3 is an operation chart of the typical library charging procedure for which the work area is shown in Figure 5-2. As an example of a repeated description, note that the activity of the right hand for both steps 15 and 16 is "Hold." During this same part of the charging cycle, the left hand is carrying out a transportation ("Move to right hand") and an operation ("Place T card in right hand").

Jobs analyzed by means of an operations chart can be improved by asking the six basic questions: Why, What, When, Where, Who, and How. The principal concern should be to eliminate unnecessary operations, and to reduce waste motion.

	SUMMARY						Library:	Johnsville
	Present		Proposed		Diff.		Department:	Circulation
	LH	RH	LH	RH	LH	RH	Operation:	Charging out a
Operation	7	9					book.	
Trans.	8	9					Operator:	R. Smith
Holds	1	2					Date:	June 1, 1966
Delays	7	3					Present	☒
Total	23	23					Proposed ☐	Sheet 1 of 1

Left Hand	Sym-bol	no.	Sym-bol	Right Hand
Idle	⟱	1	⟱	Reaches for reader's ID card.
Idle	⟱	2	◯	Picks up reader's ID card.
Idle	⟱	3	⟱	Moves card to exposure plat.
Idle	⟱	4	◯	Places card on platform.
Moves to book.	⟱	5	⟱	Moves to book.
Holds book.	▽	6	◯	Opens book.
Reaches for T-card.	⟱	7	⟱	Reaches for book card.
Picks up T-card.	◯	8	◯	Picks up book card.
Moves to exposure platform.	⟱	9	⟱	Moves to exposure platform.
Places card on platform.	◯	10	◯	Places card on platform.
Moves to left button.	⟱	11	⟱	Moves to right button.
Presses button.	◯	12	◯	Presses button.
Moves to T-card.	⟱	13	⟱	Moves to book card.
Picks up T-card.	◯	14	◯	Picks up book card.
Moves to right hand.	⟱	15	▽	Hold.
Places T-card in right hand.	◯	16	▽	Hold.
Idle.	⟱	17	⟱	Moves cards to book pocket.
Idle.	⟱	18	◯	Places cards in book pocket.
Idle	⟱	19	⟱	Moves to corner of book.
Moves to ID card.	⟱	20	◯	Closes book.
Picks up ID card.	◯	21	⟱	Idle.
Moves ID card to book.	⟱	22	⟱	Idle.
Places ID card on book.	◯	23	⟱	Idle.

Fig. 5-3 Operation chart for a charging procedure.

Some Principles of Motion Economy

Almost a half century ago the Gilbreths developed a number of principles dealing with motion economy. The greatest testimony to their contribution is that these principles have endured, largely unchanged, over the last half century. Although little used by librarians thus far, their application to highly repetitive library routines in large libraries would result in substantial benefits. Some of these principles are discussed below.

Two-Handed Work

Two-handed work is faster than one-handed; more units can be produced with less effort. The hands should begin and end motions simultaneously. The hands should not both be idle at the same time during a cycle. Motions of the arms should be made in opposite and symmetrical directions. Holds and delays should be minimized because they are not productive. For example, if the left hand is used to hold an object (cards, forms, etc.) while the right hand performs a series of operations on it, productivity would be increased if a fixture were designed to hold the object, thus freeing the left hand. A before and after illustration of two-handed work is shown in Figure 5-4.

Some view with skepticism the claims that two-handed work is faster and less fatiguing than one-handed work. A quick way to dispel doubts is to place a peg board in front of a volunteer and ask him to place a peg into each hole, working as quickly as possible using one hand. Record the time it takes to complete the task. Ask the same person to divide the pegs into two piles, one for each hand, and repeat the cycle, this time, however, using both hands to fill the peg board. The results of this little experiment are surprising -- try it. Studies have shown that people who are skilled at performing jobs with one hand will also be good at two-handed work, and those who are slow with one-handed work will probably also be slow with two-handed work.

Normal and Extended Work Areas

It is not uncommon to see a workplace, such as a desk,

Before   After

Fig. 5-4

Two alternative methods of collating sets of multiple
order slips.   The former method developed haphazard-
ly with no conscious thought to the principles of motion
economy.   The new method, on the other hand, was designed to maximize two-handed work in the normal work
area.   In addition a card rack was built and a pre-positioned fixture prepared so that the worker could employ
balanced, symetrical arm movements and develop a natural job rhythm.

bench, or table laid out incorrectly. Layouts run the gamut from
complete disorganization to arrangements in straight lines, the latter being the usual approach. Straight line layouts ignore the fact
that a person naturally works in areas bounded by arcs of circles.
Two primary work areas are the normal work area and the extended work area. The normal work area includes the surface
that can be covered by the forearms as they pivot from the elbow
with the upper arms hanging straight from the shoulders. (Area 1
in Figure 5-5). The area where the arcs overlap is the prime
working zone (Area 2 in Figure 5-5). The extended work area is
formed by arcs circumscribed by the arms extended from the
shoulders (Area 3 in Figure 5-5). The area bounded by these two
maximum arcs constitutes a zone beyond which a worker will become fatigued if work requires frequent motions into this undesirable zone. The fact that the natural motion of the arms is circu-
lar is the reason tools and equipment should be built as close as
possible around the work place.

A table arrangement illustrates clearly the difference between the normal and extended areas. The plate and silverware
occupy the central zone where most activity is concentrated. Around
the immediate periphery but in the extended zone are located the
cup and saucer, water glass, and salad bowl. Beyond that it is
customary to ask that food be passed into the "working" zones. One
can quickly appreciate the effect of a poor arrangement if he simply
reverses a place setting, that is, place the salad bowl, etc. in the
central zone and the plate in the extended area. Such a meal may
well prove more fatiguing than satisfying. Figure 5-6 illustrates a
well laid-out book discharging point at the circulation desk in a
public library.

Placement of Tools and Materials

Tools should be positioned in definite and fixed locations.
Ordinarily, when the hand is moved, the eye precedes the hand.
However, if tools and materials are pre-positioned, the hand will
automatically become accustomed to the proper location, and movements will become reflexive so that the eye can remain at the point

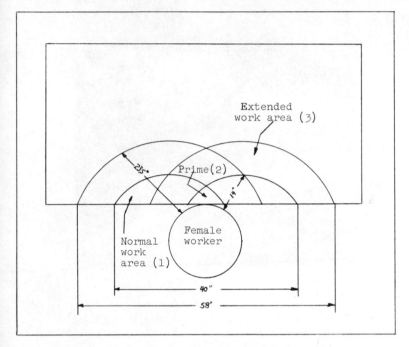

Fig. 5-5 Diagram of the dimensions of the normal
and extended work areas for a female worker.[a]

---

[a] The dimensions presented in this figure are based on data presented in Ralph Barnes, Motion and Time Study, Design and
Measurement of Work. 5th ed. (New York: Wiley, 1963), p. 260.

Fig. 5-6

Illustration of a well-laid out discharging point
at a circulation desk.

of activity.   Date cards or transaction cards located in bins at the
circulation desk illustrate this principle.   Observe an experienced
attendant charge out a book.   Her eyes will remain fixed at the
point of activity with almost no mental effort required.   (See Figure 5-7 and Figure 5-5).

Materials should be located to facilitate the best sequence
of motions.   If work is arranged in this manner, an easy and natural rhythm can be developed.   The operator is able to perform his
work with a minimum of mental effort.   In Figure 5-4, the sequence for collating multiple order forms proceeds in a systematic
fashion from top to bottom.

The Working Environment

Most libraries have provided comfortable and pleasant sur-

Fig. 5-7

Pre-positioned transaction cards.

roundings for workers. Most buildings are equipped with adequate
lighting and ventilation. Not all clerical workers, however, are
provided with a workplace suitable for the work they are expected
to perform. All too often, desks are of improper height, or are
too small, or have uncomfortable chairs. Conditions like these
can reduce morale and will reduce an individual's output.

Probably the most common difficulty in libraries is conges-
tion, with its inevitable distractions. Technical processing work
areas often give the impression of being overly cluttered. In spite
of existing standards for work area per person, libraries always
seem to be short of processing space. It is unlikely that this space
shortage will ever be eliminated. However, librarians have devised clever remedies to minimize noise and distractions. Stack
ranges, partitions, bookcases, and even files can be used to create
natural noise barriers. Workers' desks can be grouped in such a

manner as to discourage conversation.

Other Study Techniques

The techniques covered in this text will satisfy the requirements of most library studies. However, there are some special purpose techniques that deserve at least passing mention. The directions for using these tools can be found in any basic text dealing with motion and time study.

Multiple-Activity or Gang Chart

A multiple-activity chart is a flow process chart that has been modified to show processes involving the movement of more than one person or product. Figure 5-8 is an example of such a chart. These charts can be used for special situations. For example, they can be used to study the time required to transfer books en masse from one stack area to another or from one building to another when more than one person is involved. They are also applicable to inventory-taking, which is usually performed by teams. All jobs that require persons working together lend themselves to analysis with a multiple-activity chart.

Man-Machine Chart

The man-machine chart is designed to analyze the work relationships between a man and one or more machines. A machine is usually idle while it is being loaded and unloaded, and while it is in operation, the operator is often idle. It is desirable to minimize operator idle time. It may be equally important to keep machine idle time at a minimum. When the machine is rented, an idle machine will cost as much as the same machine in operation.

Use of machines in libraries is increasing. Computers with their ancillary equipment (such as keypunches) are being introduced. There has also been a widespread application of more conventional machinery -- semi-automatic typewriters, photo-duplication equipment, charging machines and pasting and labeling machines, to name but a few.

Micromotion

Many years ago Lillian Gilbreth conducted a study of the

Operation studied: Transfer of bks from old to new stacks. Seven workers using five book trucks.	Studied by: L. Jones

Library: Hillsburg Public

[X] Present [ ] Proposed

Date: 12/16/66   Sheet 1 of 1

Summary	Present	Proposed	Diff.
Total steps			
Steps/unit			

Columns: Loader, Helper, Mover #1, Mover #2, Mover #3, Unloader, Helper, Elapsed cycle time in seconds (Std.)

no.	Description
1	Loads book truck.
2	Moves truck to new stacks.
3	Unloads book truck.
4	Returns with empty truck to old stacks.
5	Waits for work.

First cycle:
(45, 90, 105, 120, 135, 150, 165, 180)

Second and all subsequent cycles:
(15, 30, 45, 60, 75, 90, 105, 120, 135)

Book trucks moved/hr. = 80

$$\% \text{ delay} = \frac{45}{900} \times \frac{100}{45} = 5$$

Fig. 5-8 Sample multiple-activity chart.

Montclair, New Jersey Public Library circulation system, employing micromotion techniques.   Micromotion study is a technique for
recording and timing an activity by means of a clock and a motion
picture camera.   The motions recorded on film were analyzed in
minute detail.   Although the study revealed ways to improve the
method, micromotion was uneconomical, and very little was accomplished that could not have been done equally well with flow
process chart analysis or operations analysis.

It is doubtful that micromotion techniques are any more applicable for library studies today than they were when Mrs. Gilbreth undertook her experiment at Montclair.   However, there is
increased interest in developing standard work times, as discussed
in Chapter XI, for routine, mechanical, library tasks.   Standard
times for basic library jobs such as pasting, dating, labeling, etc.,
could be developed under laboratory conditions.   The findings
could then be generalized, regardless of locality so long as the
standard method was followed.   In this role, micromotion study
might be useful and economically feasible.

Bibliography

American Society of Mechanical Engineers.   Operations and Flow
        Process Charts.   New York: American Society of Mechani-
        cal Engineers, 1947.   (ASME Standard 101).

Barnes, Ralph M.   Motion and Time Study.   5th ed.   New York:
        Wiley, 1963.   Chapters 8-12, 16-20.

Carson, Gordon B., ed.   Production Handbook.   New York, 1959.
        Section II, "Process Charts."

Maynard, Harold B., ed.   Industrial Engineering Handbook.   2nd
        ed.   New York: McGraw-Hill, 1963.   Section 2, "Methods;"
        Chapters 3, 5, 6 and 7.

Maynard, Harold B., and Stegemerten, G. J.   Operation Analysis.
        New York, McGraw-Hill, 1939.   Chapter 7, "The Operation
        Process Chart;" Chapter 18, "Man and Machine Process
        Charts."

Mundel, Marvin E.   Motion and Time Study.   Englewood Cliffs,
        N. J., Prentice-Hall, 1960.   Chapters 9-14.

Chapter VI
Forms: Their Analysis, Control and Design

While business has been quick to analyze its production procedures, it has been phlegmatic toward forms simplification and analysis.   This is strange indeed when one considers the multitude of forms associated with large businesses and government.   Forms are an integral part of our existence; in fact, they regulate our lives from birth certificate to death certificate.

No one really knows how much time and money are spent on the preparation and distribution of reading material.   It has been estimated that as much as twenty-five per cent of all work is in some way related to paperwork.   We do know that the number of white collar workers is steadily increasing as the number of blue collar workers declines, and that it is estimated that billions of dollars are spent each year on paper work.

Libraries are no exception; they, too, have generally done very little to control paper work.   It may be that the library profession has not yet recognized the staggering array of forms it has created.   If we were to inventory all forms used today in libraries, the list would be formidable.   To name just a few general categories, there are order request forms, multiple order forms, invoices, vouchers, reports on book funds, checking cards and kardex forms; specification cards for bindery preparation, bindery slips; card ordering forms, pre-cataloging forms, catalog correction forms; borrower's cards, date slips, transaction slips, overdues notices, reserve forms, and ILL requests. There are, of course, many varieties in each of these categories and there are many categories that have not been listed.

The opportunities for improving procedures involving paper flow are almost limitless.   The number of forms employed can be reduced either by elimination or combination of one or more forms. Assistance to library users can be improved by reducing red tape,

thus making it easier for users to obtain services and materials.
Efficiency can be improved by facilitating a freer flow of information, fixed responsibility, better outline of work methods, and reduced employee training time. The remainder of this chapter will
discuss the form process chart and its use, an outline for a forms
control program, and the basic principles of form design.

Form Process Charting

The principles of forms charting are very similar to flow
process charting. In fact, if only one form is involved, exactly
the same technique can be used with the addition of a few symbols.
Forms are usually produced in multiple copies with the various
copies being used for different purposes and travelling different
routes.   Although it would be possible to chart a copy of each form
separately, the resulting charts would be difficult to analyze. Since
the principle objective in forms charting is to produce an overview to show as simply as possible a detailed picture of the form
flow, this can best be accomplished by employing a different charting technique.

In order to understand the chart, it will first be necessary
to learn the language.   The symbols which will be used are shown
in Figure 6-1.   Remember that these symbols are no more than
tools; an analyst should feel free to alter them or add to them if
need arises.

The chart should include symbols and, when appropriate, the
distances travelled.   Descriptions should accompany those elements
that require explanation.   The information transmission symbol
(+→) necessitates an explanation as to what information was transmitted, so that the reader will know why it was transmitted.

Charting forms usually involves tracking several copies of a
form from work station to work station, department to department,
building to building, or all three.   In order to represent multiple
movement, a chart can be divided into columns, one for each work
station or other location involved, or one column for each form.
The flow of a form often proves to be circuitous and seemingly
without end.   In fact, it may become necessary to use more than

one chart. A practical solution is to enlarge the chart by attaching
a second sheet. A flow diagram (See Chapter III) is often the best
method for focusing attention on excessive movement.

When charting forms flow, it is always necessary to interview each employee involved. The part played by each employee
in the procedure should be verified and recorded. This is not always accomplished easily because a worker will occasionally have
difficulty in articulating his role.

Symbol	Name	Activity Represented
⊚	Origination	Form being made out at one work place. (No. in center represents no. of copies made).
◯	Operation	Modification of, or addition to, form at one work place.
○	Move	Change in location of form from one work place to another.
▽	Temporary Storage	Delay or waiting of form where no special order is required to perform next activity (e.g., in desk basket).
▽	Controlled Storage	Delay or waiting of form where a special order is required to perform next activity (e.g., in file cabinet).
◇	Verification	Comparison of form with other information to ascertain correctness of form.
⊹	Information Transmission	Reading or removal of information on form for use by someone or some machine.
⊠	Disposal	Form destroyed.

Fig. 6-1 Form process chart symbols.[a]

a Gerald Nadler, Work Simplification. (New York, McGraw-Hill, 1957), p. 53.

The investigator will have to be patient in drawing out pertinent facts; moreover, he will have to distinguish between fact and fiction. These words of caution should not be interpreted to mean that people will not cooperate or that they will deliberately mislead, because that is seldom the case. It is just that few people are accustomed to analyzing exactly what is done or why.

After the paper flow has been completely charted, attention can be turned to analyzing the present procedure and subsequently developing a better one. The six basic questions: Why, What, When, Where, Who, and How, as always, will prove to be the most effective approach. Check lists, such as the one which follows, will also often prove helpful.

Sample Form Check List

1. Can any form or copy be eliminated?
2. Can two or more forms be combined?
3. Can any step in the process be eliminated?
4. Is more than one administrative unit maintaining a file when one file would suffice?
5. Can forms be pre-sorted at some point during processing?
6. Can any files be eliminated? Will this form be used in the future? How often? What would be the consequences if this information were lost?
7. Can any steps be combined?
8. Can the form's originator furnish additional information?
9. Can work be eliminated by supplying copies to additional departments?
10. Can needless backtracking of forms be eliminated?
11. Can the amount of time which the form is delayed while awaiting action be reduced?

As with flow charting, there is no substitute for an inquiring mind. No check list will supplant curiosity or the skill of a practiced forms analyst.

Illustration

To illustrate how forms processing can help, let us use this technique to trace an order request card and order multiforms from their inception until all actions have been completed and all forms have either been filed or destroyed. The original procedure is shown in Figure 6-2. Bottlenecks and delays occurred frequently in the Receiving Section. Copies of each order were filed in three locations before an order was sent to a vender; and likewise, three files were cleared when a book arrived. The terminal file, which was an inventory of books received and processed, was not related directly to processing, but it did require order section personnel for upkeep.

The new procedure (See Figure 6-3) was designed to eliminate processing bottlenecks. Two files were combined, one eliminated, and one altered (the date file) so that it was consulted only when all other access avenues failed. Finally, the chart revealed that information on the order card was not being utilized effectively. All bibliographic and order information collected by the requester and acquisitions personnel, some of which would have been useful to the cataloging department, was recorded; but since the card was retained permanently in Acquisitions, the information was never utilized. The revised procedure was designed so that the original order card accompanied the book it represented throughout processing. Upon completion of processing, the order card was returned to Acquisitions so that the in-process record could be cleared; the card was then returned to the original requester as his notification that the book was ready for use.

A Forms Control Program

The first step of a control program is to inventory all of an organization's forms. How many of us can report accurately the number of forms presently in use in his library department? It might be useful to try an experiment. Estimate the number of forms now in use. Then search in every nook and cranny until each form actually in use has been found. The number will probably far exceed your estimate. An estimate made by one of the authors was exceeded by three hundred per cent, which was the first indication that something needed to be done.

Once collected, the forms should be classified by function. Some businesses have established very elaborate classification and coding schemes for this purpose which are analogous to book subject classification schemes such as Dewey or Library of Congress. The intent is to relate forms according to organizational functions,

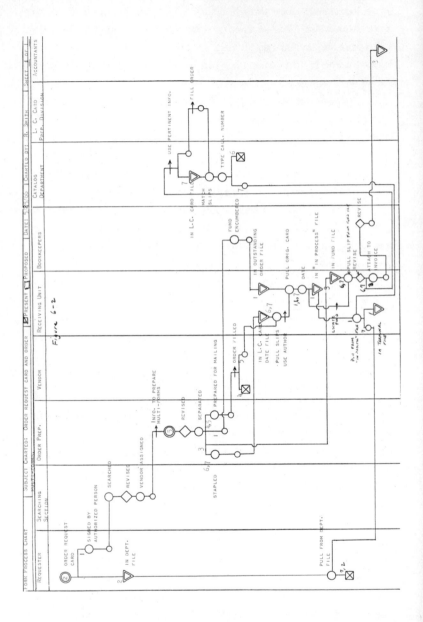

Figure 6-2

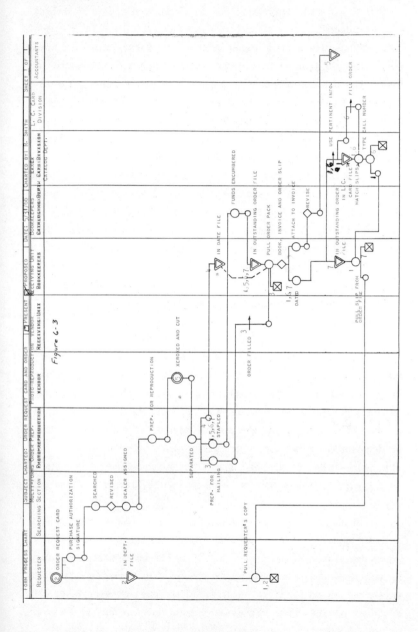

Figure 6-3

so that undesirable duplication can be eliminated and relationships
can be detected.

Evaluating a form's essentiality calls for careful thought and
frequently will require interviews and meetings with interested parties.   The basic problem is to identify and define information essential to an organization, as distinguished from information which
is useful but not essential and from information that is unnecessary.
A committee composed of department heads or their representatives
should be in a position to know what each department is doing and
would, therefore, be able to relate each department's efforts to the
work of the others.   Persuading departments to give up information which they are used to receiving will present a challenge; and
even reaching a group concensus may not always be routine.   But
it is essential at an early stage to pinpoint the reason for each
form, whether it is a new or an old form.

Information once essential to an organization may have become outmoded by changing needs, but because no one has taken
the trouble of re-evaluating the need, the information is still rou-
tinely produced, disseminated and probably filed.

In much the same way that a systems analyst approaches
the study of procedures, a forms survey should be undertaken first
in those areas that promise the greatest gains: for example, departments utilizing the most forms, departments with the greatest
number of employees, departments experiencing work bottlenecks,
or departments using forms which are obviously unnecessary.   Finally, for pragmatic reasons, it is often advantageous to begin a
study in a department that is receptive to the idea of a forms survey.

In business it is common for the forms control person and
systems' person to work independently.   The former turns a completed form over to the latter, and it is the latter's responsibility
to assimilate the form into a new system.   In libraries this would
rarely be possible.   Most libraries do not have personnel specially
assigned to either task, let alone to both.   Consequently, whoever
is responsible for management studies will probably also be responsible for forms.

The logical conclusion of a forms control inventory is to establish central forms control. One person or section should be given the responsibility for drawing up forms and for revising, preserving, reproducing, and distribution. A central unit is in an advantageous position to prevent unnecessary forms proliferation by maintaining a continuing and functional forms inventory. But it can happen that a central forms unit becomes a bottleneck. If a forms unit develops a reputation for delaying work people will begin to look for ways to by-pass it. If a unit needs a new form, it will not appreciate delay resulting from evaluation by a forms unit. It is essential that every effort be made to maintain close and amicable relations with other departments. Even if a department submits a form that appears to be inefficient or poorly designed, it may be better to reproduce it in small quantity, enough to allow the department to operate, and then later to make arrangements for perfecting or elimination of the form.

Throughout the preceeding paragraphs we have alluded to a person or unit responsible for forms control and design. At some point this responsibility will have to be delegated to someone in the library. There are no hard and fast rules. A good beginning might be to appoint a committee to examine existing forms. This group might also be responsible for evaluating new forms. The program might be assigned to the business manager, an administrative assistant, or a staff member who possesses special qualifications. There is no one best approach; it will be governed in part by local circumstances and the size of the library.

Most libraries will continue to rely on library supply catalogs for their forms. Because of this, it should be noted that inclusion of a form in a supplier's catalog does not guarantee efficacy nor does it guarantee need. For example, detailed statistical sheets are not needed if a library finds a very simple statistical record satisfactory. Forms listed in such catalogs, by and large, represent what libraries have requested and have used over the years. These forms are standard in format and may, perhaps be used successfully by most libraries. But a library will have to exercise judgment as to which forms apply to its particular circumstances.

Retention of Forms and Records

This chapter will not discuss in detail the principles of a records retention program. This topic is covered adequately in other texts.

Little attention has been paid to the question of how long or how many of a library's records should be retained. Consider the libraries that continue indiscriminately to maintain accession books and multiple registration files, or that retain for years and years records of all books on which processing has been completed. In isolated instances, when required by local legal or fiscal regulations, certain records may be necessary; but in most cases they are not.

The basic criterion for records retention is the question of cost of maintenance and housing versus frequency of use as against the penalty incurred if a form is needed after it has been destroyed. Predicting future needs is not always easy. If in some cases a decision must be deferred, it should be reconsidered at a later date. All files and records should be reviewed periodically. Time will often alter informational needs, which in turn will affect retention requirements. It is axiomatic that as the quantity of records increases, so does the cost of retention in terms of floor space, equipment, and labor.

Forms Design

An effective form can be a great aid in gathering, processing, communicating, and recording information. It is, therefore, important that every attempt be made to design the best possible form. Once in use, a form can become either a source of savings or of waste. Some libraries have given considerable attention to forms design. There are many forms in use today that reflect careful thought and planning.

A few guides for the neophyte designer are listed below:

1. Before actually drawing the layout, it is first wise to allocate space by typing the form's information requirements. After the width of each space is measured in tenths of an inch,

the total space requirements can be established. Space for mar-
gins must not be forgotten. If the necessary space is lacking
after calculating the total needs, either allocations for some
boxes can be reduced, or a larger form can be used. A form
with inadequate space will probably prove unsuccessful, or at
least difficult to read because answers will be cramped and il-
legible.

    2. Use standard size forms such as 3 x 5, 4 x 6, 5 x 8, or
8. 5 x 11 inches. Odd sizes usually cost more to produce and
are more difficult to store.

    3. Spacing between lines will depend on the method in which
the form will be filled out by those who use it. Normally 1/4"
is allowed for handwritten entries and 1/3" for typewritten entries, but when space is at a premium, these allocations can be
reduced to 1/5" for handwritten and 1/6" for typewritten entries.

    4. Arrange items so that writing proceeds from left to right
and from top to bottom. On some forms, it is also possible to
order the items so that the most frequently required blocks are
located first. Entries should be laid out in the same sequence
as the data which is to be transcribed is listed on the work
sheet. Group common information (i. e. , all information used by
one person or department) in blocks.

    5. Align boxes vertically to reduce the need for tab stops on
the typewriter.

    6. Whenever possible, use the box design with descriptive
captions in the upper left-hand corner, i. e. , Name̲̅ ̲̅ ̲̅ ̲̅ .
This form is usually superior to that which uses captions followed by a dotted line, i. e. , Name . . . .

    7. Pre-print as much information as possible. This will re-
duce completion time for users.

    8. Consider using different type faces, heavy rules, shaded
areas or different colors to give certain areas or information
special emphasis.

    9. Give each form a number and a title that is descriptive
of its function. A form number will facilitate easy identification
and retrievability. The date of preparation should also be in-

cluded either as part of the I. D. number or separately. A
date provides the form analyst with a signal for periodic revision.

10. Whenever possible, place instructions for filling out directly on the form. They should precede the section to which
they apply. The reverse side of the form also can be used for
complicated instructions.

11. Use symbols and abbreviations only when there can be
no misunderstanding as to their meaning.

12. Design forms so that mailing addresses are located to
fit window envelopes. Have space for addressee and addressor
if the form is a traveler.

In some instances it will prove advantageous to use a pilot
run before a form is printed in its final form. A prototype can be
drawn and a small sample reproduced. The samples can then be
distributed to a few selected users. Failings of the form exposed
during the trial run can then be corrected in the final version. A
trial period might not always be practical because of the time delay; but whenever practical, a trial period should be employed,
since even the most experienced forms design specialist will occasionally let a blunder slip through.

Types of Forms

Form letters should be used whenever possible. Librarians
still hesitate to use them perhaps because they feel that form letters frequently do not fit the problem perfectly. Most institutions
which libraries deal with will be satisfied if the correspondence
they receive is intelligible and legible regardless of format. There
is a growing trend for businesses to scrawl answers on original letters. This is an obvious time saver even if esthetically offen-
sive. Speed letters employing NCR (no carbons required) paper or
preinserted carbons are also finding acceptance. These multi-part
forms are designed in a manner similar to an inter-office memo-
randum. The originator sends two copies to the recipient and retains the third copy for his files. The recipient prepares his answer and returns the second copy. He retains the original as his

permanent record of the communications.

Forms have been developed in all shapes and sizes for almost every conceivable use.   Anyone who has ever examined library forms will quickly conclude that library forms are no exception.   There are single-sheet forms, continuous forms, multi-part
forms, tag forms, marginal punch cards and internal punched
cards, computor printouts, etc.   Multi-part forms have made a major impact on library operation because of their tremendous time
saving potential.   These forms can be purchased as single units,
in continuous rolls with perforations, or continuous rolls with marginal punches to be used in machines equipped with forms-feed devices.   The use of tractor pins and marginally punched forms insures accurate alignment from copy to copy and set to set.   This
can become critical when six or more copies are produced.

The Evolution of a Form

One of the forms most frequently used in libraries is the
book order request.   Some libraries use 50,000 to 75,000 or more
of these cards each year.   During the last seven or eight years,
the form used at the University of North Carolina at Chapel Hill
has been revised six times.   The changes represent both changing
institutional needs and attempts to improve the form.   Most of the
changes took place without consideration of form design principles,
which might suggest that much of what has been said can eventually be learned through trial and error.   However, this is hardly the
most efficient procedure.

The form shown in Figure 6-4 was the first version.   It
was designed primarily for the requester.   Once the card arrived
in the library, all additional information was written in by hand.
For example, all information concerning added copies (AC), editions (AE), and volumes (AV) had to be written on the back.   All
bibliographical searching information including the search of the order file and catalog also had to be written out.

48 - 9571

Author ....Lowell, James Russell.. k ᶜ
(Surname first)
Title ...✓ ͤssays, poems and letters, selected and edited
          by William Smith Clark II   / ᶜ
....
                                                                              k ᶜ
....

Place .... Vols................
Publisher ....Odyssey Press.............................. Price.. 2.50
Date Published ..1948... Cost............
Recommended by ....Essay and gen lit index
Charged to ....Dept.

Fig. 6-4 Original Form

Author_____ O
(Surname first)   K
Title_____   L
_____   P

_____ Copies_____
Place_____ Vols. _____
Publisher_____ Price_____
Date Published_____ Edition_____ _____
Recommended by_____
Charged to_____ Dept.

Fig. 6-5 First Revision

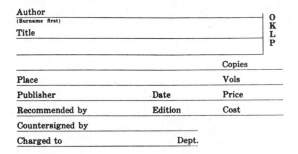

Fig. 6-6 Second Revision

Form revisions one and two did not really represent changes in philosophy, but rather slight refinements, of the form. (See Figures 6-5 and 6-6). Both revisions provided space for the bibliographic searcher to record whether or not the order file, card catalog, and Library of Congress bibliographies had been searched and whether the search uncovered any information. The information located still had to be written out in longhand. Space was provided for requesting specific editions and for an authorization signature.

Revision three (Figure 6-7) illustrates a significant change in the order request card. This version utilized box entries instead of captions followed by lines. More pre-printed information was included. More important, space was provided for recording not only the basic bibliographic facts, but also the source of a request if it originated from a dealers' catalog. The card also provided space for indicating if a request was for a book already owned by the library; an edition of a title already owned, part of a series, or a replacement of a lost title (RP). Finally, space was provided for recording an L. C. Card Number, and for showing when a book was ordered and when it was received.

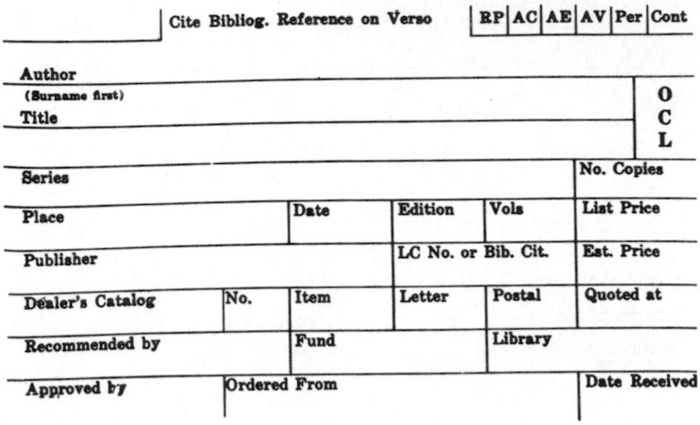

Cite Bibliog. Reference on Verso | RP | AC | AE | AV | Per | Cont

Author
(Surname first)
Title

O
C
L

Series | No. Copies
Place | Date | Edition | Vols | List Price
Publisher | LC No. or Bib. Cit. | Est. Price
Dealer's Catalog | No. | Item | Letter | Postal | Quoted at
Recommended by | Fund | Library
Approved by | Ordered From | Date Received

Fig. 6-7 Third Revision

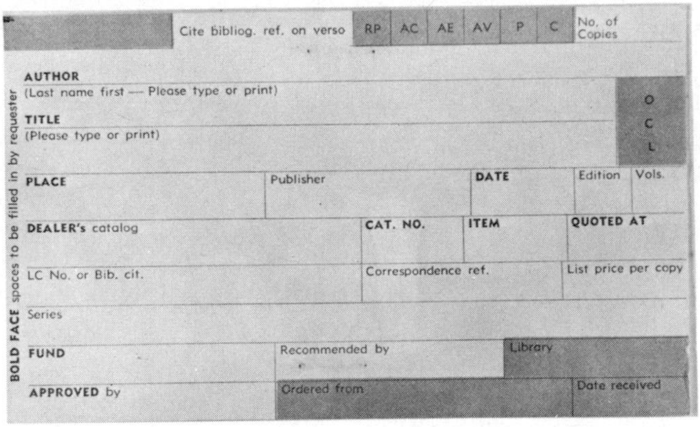

Cite bibliog. ref. on verso | RP | AC | AE | AV | P | C | No. of Copies

AUTHOR
(Last name first — Please type or print)
TITLE
(Please type or print)

O
C
L

PLACE | Publisher | DATE | Edition | Vols.
DEALER's catalog | CAT. NO. | ITEM | QUOTED AT
LC No. or Bib. cit. | Correspondence ref. | List price per copy
Series
FUND | Recommended by | Library
APPROVED by | Ordered from | Date received

BOLD FACE spaces to be filled in by requester

Fig. 6-8 Fourth Revision

The fourth revision was basically a refined version of the third with two important exceptions.   For the first time, the spacing of lines was set to typewriter spacing, that is, six lines to the inch.   All of its predecessors were spaced at four lines per inch, which was not easy to use in a typewriter.   This version of the order card also attempted to improve the quality and completeness of bibliographical information supplied by requesters by distinguishing between those blocks to be filled in by the requester from those to be filled in by library personnel.   This was done by shading certain areas of the card.

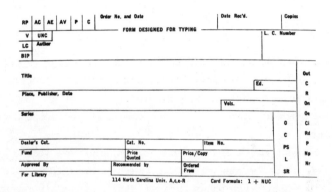

Fig. 6-9 Fifth Revision -- Recto

Revision five (Figures 6-9 and 6-10) represents a radical departure from its predecessors.   It was designed to serve the triple function of request card, purchase order form and L. C. card order form.   The information blocks were arranged so that bibliographic information was typed in the same order that would later be used in transcribing it onto a catalog card.   For the first time, information was pre-printed on the verso of the card.   (See Figure 6-10).   It was now possible for the bibliographical searchers to re-

Call Number of Requested Book	Series		LC	DB	Your Request has been Returned Because:
	Class & Cat Sep		LCS	JVZ	
	Make Series a.e.		LC 48—	OB	☐ Library Already Owns Title
			NUC 53—	SchB	
	Class Together		NUC 58—	Fichero	☐ A copy has been ordered for:
	Analyzed		NUC —	L. Esp	
	Author		PW —	L. K.	☐ Library will receive title on standing order
	Au-t		BPR —	N. K.	
Call No. of AC, AE, or AV in Library	Full		CBI	MIRA	
	Not Analyzed		PTLA	NYPL-SC	Publisher has cancelled our order:
			BM	Other	
	Ser. Rec.	Cat.	BM Sub.		___Out-of-print
	Ulrich		BM2		___Out-of-stock
	ULS		BNB		___Sold
	NST		H-L		___Unavailable
Date Order Recd in Acquisitions			BIBLIO		If you wish library to advertise, indicate below. Return this card to the ACQ Dept.
			BIB. Fr.		
Bibliographic Source of Request			BN		☐ Advertise

Form No. 851

Fig. 6-10 Fifth Revision -- Verso

cord efficiently where they had searched and the results of each
search.   Space was also provided for searching for series and in-
forming a serials cataloger of prior decisions.   Finally, the form
provided space to inform a requester when his order had been cancelled and why.

Revision five was in use for approximately one year.   Like
its predecessors, it was not without defects.   In an effort to include as much information as possible, the form became cluttered.
This was especially true of the verso, where many of the boxes
were assigned to specific bibliographies, and where the space for
series information and the block used to inform a requester that
his order had been cancelled by the vender were rarely used. The
blocks to report a duplicate order were not used because of inadequate space.

In revision six, which is the version currently in use, a compromise was made between constant information and variable information.   The major change on the recto was to include the mailing
address of the Acquisitions Department of the Library.   For some
reason this essential bit of information (essential because the form
is used as a purchase order) was heretofore overlooked.   It was

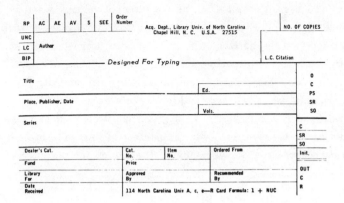

Fig. 6-11 Sixth Revision -- Recto

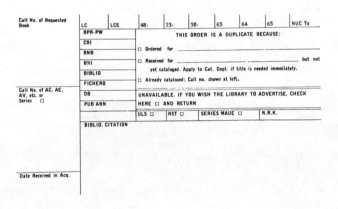

Fig. 6-12 Sixth Revision -- Verso

also possible, through correspondence with the Library of Congress, to reduce from ten to three the L. C. Card Division report symbols

of the previous draft. An effort has been made to correct the
shortcomings on the verso of the previous draft.

To regard revision six as the ultimate version would be
wishful thinking. Even now, automation and the changes it will
bring loom on the horizon. It has also been suggested that since
every individual or departmental librarian requesting new books
keeps a file of his orders, it would be more economical, in the
long run, to use a two-part multiform with the second copy made
of NCR paper. This would be of great help to a requester and
would be an improvement over the present method of using P-slips
and carbon paper. So, very likely, the search for the ultimate
form will continue.

Bibliography

Knox, Frank M. Design and Control of Business Forms. New
    York: McGraw-Hill, 1952. (NOMA Series in Office Man-
    agement).

Lazarro, Victor, ed. Systems and Procedures: a Handbook for
    Business and Industry. New York: Prentice-Hall, 1959.
    Chapter 8, "Forms Design and Control;" Chapter 9, "Rec-
    ords Management."

Littlefield, Cleatice L. , and Rachel, Frank. Office and Adminis-
    trative Mangement. 2nd ed. Englewood Cliffs, N. J. :
    Prentice-Hall, 1964. Chapter 16, "Forms Design and Con-
    trol."

Mundel, Marvin E. Motion and Time Study. 3rd ed. Englewood
    Cliffs, N. J. : Prentice-Hall, 1960. Chapter 8, "Process
    Chart-Combined Analysis."

Nadler, Gerald. Work Simplification. New York: McGraw-Hill,
    1957. Chapter 5, "Forms Process Chart."

U. S. Bureau of the Budget. Simplifying Procedures Through Forms
    Control. Washington, D. C. : U. S. Government Printing Of-
    fice, 1948. (Management Bulletin, June, 1948).

Chapter VII
Time Study

The Value of Time Study

Time study is a technique for determining the time required by a qualified, well-trained person working at a normal pace to do a specified job. It is a form of work measurement. Time study is an activity which follows logically after an analysis of the existing job and the elimination of unnecessary steps (motion study). The standard methods for making motion analysis have been covered in previous chapters.

Before plunging into the details of time study, some of its uses should be considered. Time study data can be used to determine time standards. These figures can then be used to establish fair and reasonable performance standards. Performance standards, their construction and usefulness, are discussed in detail in Chapter XI. Secondly, time study data are necessary to calculate the costs of a system. A budget with its cost estimates based on work measurement data will be a more accurate and supportable document than one with cost estimates based on guesswork. Finally, time study, through standards, enables administrators to gauge employee performance -- to reward above standard performance, to give those who need it such additional training as required to achieve the standard and, when necessary, to take disciplinary action.

Making a Time Study

Time Study Equipment

For library time studies an ordinary wrist watch is usually all that is needed. The watch should have a clearly visible second hand. In industry, where many jobs require more precise timing than do many library operations, it is standard procedure to use a stop watch. A stop watch should, for convenience of computation, have a decimally divided face (See Figure 7-1). It need not be a

99

heavy investment.   As with ordinary watches, there is a wide price range.   A good quality watch that reads to 1/100 minute and will total up to 60 minutes may be obtained for as little as $25. 00 to $30. 00.   There are numerous stop watch manufacturers listed in Thomas' Register of American Manufacturers.

Fig. 7-1 Decimal-Minute Stop Watch

Time study men in industry sometimes record times by means of motion picture cameras and even more sophisticated devices.   The choice of equipment depends on the nature of the job and the degree of accuracy required.   The accuracy required depends to a large extent on the frequency with which a job is performed.   A small error in a task requiring a small amount of time, projected a million times will result in a substantial miscalculation; the same job performed only a few thousand times does not require the same degree of timing accuracy.   It is worth emphasizing that most library time studies can be performed successfully with an ordinary watch with a sweep second hand.

Professional time study people generally use decimal stop watches and record their times to the nearest hundredth of a minute.   A librarian may have available only an ordinary watch with a

sexagesimal face, or even a stop watch so divided (perhaps borrowed or begged from the Athletic Department). It is not wrong to
time in minutes and seconds. It is, however less convenient for
decimal computation. In any case, it is an easy matter to convert
from seconds to hundredths of a minute and vice versa by using the
following formulas:

Hundredths of a minute = 5/3 x Seconds

Seconds = 3/5 x Hundredths of a minute

For example, 16.2 seconds would be equivalent to 5/3 x 16.2, or
27 hundredths of a minute; 27 hundredths of a minute would be
equivalent to 3/5 x 27, or 16.2 seconds.

If many such computations must be made, a conversion table
is a convenience. Such tables are at hand in any library. For example, in the mathematical tables section of any edition of the ubiq-
uitous Handbook of Chemistry and Physics one will find together a
table of "Minutes and seconds to decimal parts of a degree" and one
of "Decimal parts of a degree to minutes and seconds." Or conversions may be made conveniently on the slide rule.

In addition to a timing device, the person making the study
will want some sort of clipboard to hold the paper on which he records his observations. Special observation boards that are designed to hold both paper and stop watch in a convenient position
can be purchased for about $10.00 (See Figure 7-2). Special time
study forms may also be purchased; or the analyst may devise his
own (See Figure 7-4). Slide rules and calculating machines are
useful for lessening the time and drudgery of computation. Even if
a librarian does not happen to have a calculator in his department,
there is almost always one he can use in the library office or in
some other nearby office. A librarian can learn all he needs to
know about the slide rule -- namely, how to multiply and divide --
in only a few minutes. The basic instructions for using a slide
rule are covered in Chapter IX.

Developing a Standard Method

The customary procedure for an industrial methods analyst
is to develop a standard procedure before undertaking a time study.

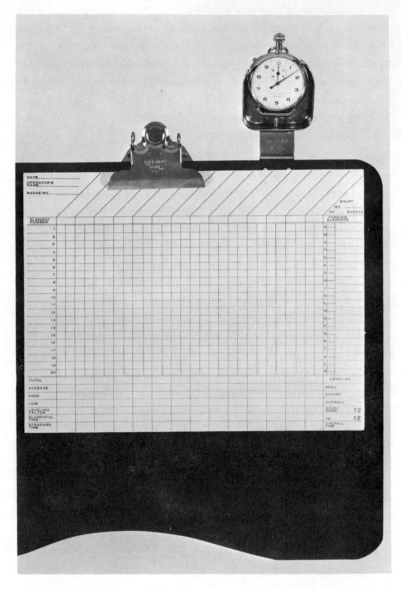

Fig. 7-2 Observation Board With Stop Watch
and Observation Sheet for Recording Times

The reason for this is that if the original procedure is later modified, the timing operations will have to be repeated.   Of course,
developing a standard method is one of the purposes of motion
study and accounts for the fact that motion study v sually preceeds
time study.

It is usually necessary, since libraries do not generally
know their costs, to chart the present procedure and collect times
so as to provide a basis for comparison when new methods are
studied.

Dividing the Job to be Timed Into Elements

The standard job description must next be broken into ob-
servable elements which may be easily timed.   In industrial situations experience has shown that observations more than 30 seconds
in duration tend to become inaccurate.   For most library studies,
however, such a high degree of precision is not necessary.   This
is fortunate because in many library processes the most natural
and convenient elements to time can run as long as several minutes in duration.   However, every effort should be made to keep
the time of each element as short as possible.

For ease of timing, the elements should be divided in such
a way that the analyst will be able to tell readily when one element
ends and another begins, either by sight or sound.   An analyst
should also separate out those elements that are not controlled by
the operator.   For example, a study of a Xerox 914 in operation
would require two types of elements: The cycle time of the machine, and the handling time of the operator.

Finally, constant elements should be distinguished from variable elements; that is, those elements which do not experience time
fluctuations from cycle to cycle should be separated from those elements that experience large cyclical fluctuations.   Although it is
very common in the metal industries for processes to include pre-
dominately constant elements, the reverse is true in libraries.   In
industrial environs it is customary to define a constant element as
one that is free from the influences of size, weight, length, and
shape.   To these four factors, an additional variable must be

added, that of human interaction.   Numerous library routines involve dialogues between two or more individuals -- for example,
registering a new reader or collecting fine money.   Such interactions produce cyclical variations.   This is not a serious problem;
all that is required are additional observations to offset the extra
variation.   The number of observations required is discussed in
Chapter VIII.

Selecting the Person to be Timed

There may be two or more persons performing the same
operation either simultaneously or at different times of the day.   As
an example of the former, several persons are likely to be typing
or filing at the same time; as an example of the latter, the person
manning a charging machine during the evening hours may not be
the same person who worked the afternoon shift.   In choosing an
operator to be timed, it usually makes sense to time one who regularly works at a normal pace, rather than either the high producer
or the low producer.   If the fastest worker is timed, there is a
risk that other employees may view the study findings with suspi-
cion.

Taking the Times

There are two common ways to record time data.   One is
to let the watch run continuously.   The person doing the timing
merely records the time reading at the end of each element in the
appropriate space on his data sheet.   The actual time for each element is determined later by subtraction (See Figure 7-4).   This
method does not require a stop watch.   It has the disadvantage of
requiring a good deal of subtraction.   The second method, commonly known as "snapback," requires a stop watch.   Stop watches are
so constructed that, at any time, by pressing the stem of the watch,
the hands may be snapped back to zero.   At the end of each element, the observer reads his watch, snaps the watch hand back to
zero, and then records the time for the element he has just read
(See Figure 7-3).   The advantage to this method is that the times
are recorded directly, thus eliminating the need for subtraction,
and allowing the person timing to see more easily variations in

time values while he is still on the job.   There are other less
commonly used techniques beyond the two described in which two,
and even three, stop watches are used.   The interested reader will
find descriptions of these methods in the books listed in the chapter
bibliography.

Recording the Readings

To a beginner it might not seem possible to observe an operator, read a watch, and record time readings almost simultaneously;
but with practice he will discover that timing a worker is not at all
difficult.   The first rule in timing a job is to observe and record
each phase of the job.   Occasionally the analyst will observe an
element that occurs only infrequently.   For example, a circulation
discharging routine does not ordinarily include collecting fine money
for overdue books, but the time required to collect fines should be
recorded.   Additional watch readings will have to be collected for
infrequently performed elements in order to have sufficient data.
In addition, it will be necessary to establish the frequency of occurrence of the elements that do not appear in every cycle so that
their times can be prorated.

An analyst will also be confronted with a third type of element
-- the foreign element.   A foreign element is one that does not occur regularly in the cycle, such as a reader dropping his ID card
while presenting it to the desk attendant.   Times for foreign elements should be recorded during the observations.   They may be
ignored later if they happen so infrequently and involve so little total time as to be insignificant.

Time Study of a Binding Preparation Process

A study of a library binding preparation process will illustrate
the essentials of making a time study.   The standard procedure was
divided into six elements (See Figure 7-4).   1) The bindery clerk
pulled the binding specification card for each title to be bound.   2)
Next, using the specification card as a guide, he recorded on the
bindery slip such information as the volume number, index and TPI
(title page index) placement, disposition of covers and ads and so
forth.   This was done by hand, so most of the recording consisted

no.	Element	1	2	3	4	5	6	7	8	9	10
1	Pull bindery spec. card	.65	.80	.60	.83	.82	.87	.68	.60	.65	.73
2	Write info. on bindery slip	1.40	1.52	1.67	1.72	1.45	1.26	1.34	1.52	1.67	1.15
3	Type info. on bindery slip	.92	.73	.87	.92	.78	1.15	.85	.68	.73	.72
4	Inspection of typing	.45	.20	.33	.31	.40	.27	.38	.47	.48	.53
5	Stamp T-no. on bindery slip	.10	.07	.08	.09	.10	.08	.10	.08	.09	.10
6	Refile spec. card	.55	.48	.57	.63	.70	.67	.68	.55	.56	.67

Fig. 7-3 Example of repetitive or snap-back method of timing.

merely of checking boxes.   3) Then he typed the title and call number on the bindery slip.   4) Next, he inspected his typing. [1]   5)
Then, using a Bates numbering machine, he stamped a transaction
number onto the slip.   6) Finally, he refiled the specification card
into the master file.   The completed slip was then put with the material to be bound and sent to a commercial binder. [2]

     The time observation sheet (Figure 7-4) summarizes the
time observations for ten cycles.   The continuous method of timing
was employed.   The procedure for calculating the times for each
element per cycle, the total elemental times for each of the ten
cycles, and the average observed time for each element are calculated in the following manner.   The analyst observes the operator
until the end of an element is reached.   He then reads his watch
and records the time on the time study observation sheet in the box
labelled "R" ("Reading") for the first element in cycle one (in the
binding example this reading is 0. 65 minutes).   At the end of the
second element the analyst records the watch reading in the "R"
box for element two, cycle one (2. 05 minutes).   This procedure is
continued until the last element in the cycle has been observed and
the time recorded (4. 07 minutes).   The stop watch hands are
snapped back to zero and the observation process started again for
cycle two.

     Once the observations for all of the cycles have been re-
corded, the elemental times in each cycle are computed by a process of subtraction.   The time for the first element is correct as
recorded on the observation sheet and thus is written without subtraction in the "T" ("Time") box.   In the illustration this value of
0. 65 minutes for element one is subtracted from the reading for
element two (2. 05 - 0. 65 = 1. 40 minutes).   To obtain the elemental
time for three, the reading for element two is subtracted from the
reading for three (2. 97 - 2. 05 = 0. 92 minutes).   This subtraction
procedure is continued until the elemental times for all cycles have
been calculated.   The next step is to add the times for each element and record the sums in the TOT (total) column.   Finally, the
totals are divided by the number of observations -- which yields
the average elemental times.   This is recorded in the AVG (aver-

TIME STUDY OBSERVATION SHEET																
Operation Preparing bindery slips for periodicals.								**Allowances** 12 %								
Time started 8:30 **Time finished** 11:10								**Std Time** 5.84 min.								
Observer J. Jones **Date** 10/10/66								**Units/hr.** 82.4								

no.	Elements		1	2	3	4	5	6	7	8	9	10	ΣT	T̄	RF	NT
1	Pull bindery spec. card from file.	T	.65	.80	.68	.83	.82	.87	.68	.60	.65	.73	7.31	.73		
		R	.65	.80	.68	.83	.82	.87	.68	.60	.65	.73				
2	Write info. on bindery slip.	T	1.40	1.52	1.67	1.72	1.45	1.26	1.34	1.52	1.67	1.15	14.70	1.47		
		R	2.05	2.32	2.35	2.55	2.27	2.13	2.02	2.12	2.32	1.88				
3	Type info. on bindery slip.	T	.92	.73	.87	.92	.78	1.15	.85	.68	.73	.72	8.35	.83		
		R	2.97	3.05	3.22	3.47	3.05	3.28	2.87	2.80	3.05	2.60				
4	Inspection of typing.	T	.45	.20	.33	.31	.40	.27	.38	.47	.48	.53	3.82	.38		
		R	3.42	3.25	3.55	3.78	3.45	3.55	3.25	3.27	3.53	3.13				
5	Stamp T-no. on bindery slip.	T	.10	.07	.08	.09	.10	.08	.10	.08	.09	.10	.89	.09		
		R	3.52	3.32	3.63	3.87	3.55	3.63	3.35	3.35	3.62	3.23				
6	Refile spec. card in file.	T	.55	.48	.57	.63	.70	.67	.68	.55	.56	.67	6.06	.61		
		R	4.07	3.80	4.20	4.50	4.25	4.30	4.03	3.90	4.18	3.90				
7		T														
		R														
8		T														
		R														
9		T														
		R														
10		T														
		R														
11		T														
		R														
12		T														
		R														
13		T														
		R														
14		T														
		R														
15		T														
		R														
16		T														
		R														
17		T														
		R														
18		T														
		R														
19		T														
		R														
20		T														
		R														
	TOTALS													4.11	1.25	5.14

Fig. 7-4 Sample time study observation sheet.

age) column. For example, for element one the total time is 7.31
minutes and the average time is 7.31/10, or 0.73 minutes.

Determining How Many Observations Are Necessary

One of the first questions a neophyte time analyst is likely
to ask is: "How many observations should I make: two, five, ten,
twenty-five, one hundred; just when can I stop?" The question is
pertinent because if too few observations are taken, the data collected is likely to be unreliable; on the other hand, if too many observations are taken, study costs will be increased needlessly.
Therefore, what the analyst is interested in determining is the minimum number of observations to produce data with sufficient reliability to satisfy his study requirements. As long as his needs are
met, the method employed to gather the data is of secondary importance.

The magnitude of variation in the times from cycle to cycle
correlates directly with the number of readings that will have to be
gathered. As variation increases so will be the number of readings
required. For example, if an analyst were to time a call number
labelling process and the times (in minutes) for just ten cycles
proved to be .55, 1.22, .32, 1.13, 1.30, .44, .72, .43, .82, and
.62, could the analyst state with certainty that the average of .75
minutes is truly representative? If the answer is no, then additional readings would be required. On the other hand, if the observed times had been .69, .81, .75, .85, .68, .72, .76, .84,
.64, and .89 which yields the same average .75, the analyst could
have been more confident that .75 minutes actually was a representative average even though he still did not know the exact number of
readings he should record.

Statisticians have developed a simple formula for calculating
an adequate sample size. This procedure is described in Chapter
VIII. When this approach is used, an analyst will have a solid
foundation for substantiating the validity of the study. However,
there will be occasions when the precision that statistical technique
can provide is unwarranted, and in such cases a simpler common
sense approach will prove equally satisfactory. For example, ten

observations of a charging process might yield the following times:
. 10, . 08, . 07, . 08, . 09, . 10, . 09, . 11, . 12, and . 11. The average for these times is 0. 095 minutes. Suppose we had some mys-
tic power and learned later that the correct average time for charging out a book was 0. 11 minutes. Our study is 0. 02 minutes in
error, but would an error of this magnitude have proven critical?
For the vast majority of libraries the answer would be no.

Although the example in the preceding paragraph was not
contrived, it was at least convenient. An analyst will not always
be so fortunate as to have a definite pattern emerge so quickly. In
an actual study, what must be done is to continue recording times
until one is satisfied that a truly representative pattern has
emerged. This prgmatic approach can be checked by the formula
given in Chapter VIII.

Rating the Worker

If a time study analyst were to calculate work standards and
costs on the basis of observed times, the results would be completely misleading. Costs would be underestimated and production
overestimated. It is necessary to adjust observed times so that
they reflect reality. Industrial time analysts have devised elaborate methods for this purpose. This procedure is called "rating the
worker." A worker under observation tends to work at a faster
pace than he would normally work. The chief reasons for this are
nervousness and job motivation, both of which stem from being
singled out for special attention.

At this point it is natural to ask what is "normal?" Normal
time is the time it will take a qualified person working at a normal
pace and using a standardized method to perform a job. The rating
process itself consists of adjusting the observed speed to the time
analyst's conception of normal speed. This adjustment is based on
the judgment of the analyst and is therefore subjective. Consequently, regardless of the elaborate systems employed, rating cannot be carried out with mechanical precision. The accuracy of
rating depends almost entirely upon the skill and judgment of the
rater and on what appears fair to the employee.

There are several rating methods now in use.   Here only
the commonest will be described.   The reader is referred to the
chapter bibliography for information on the others.   While the analyst is collecting time observations, he is also evaluating the operator's skill, effort, and speed.   If the analyst judges the operator's
speed to be equal to the "Theoretical normal," he assigns a rating
of 100%; if the observed speed is thought to be less than normal,
a rating of less than 100% is given; or if the worker's pace is
judged faster than normal, a rating of more than 100% is assigned.
The percentage rating factor, expressed as a decimal or fraction,
is multiplied by the average observed time to obtain the normal
time.

The formula for computing normal time is:

Normal Time (N_T) = Observed Time (O_T) x Rating Factor (RF)

The binding preparation time study will help illustrate the
use of this formula.   In that study the analyst judged that the
worker was working much faster than his normal pace.   Overall he
estimated that the worker was producing approximately 25 per cent
above normal; therefore, he assigned a rating factor of 1.25.   The
normal time was then calculated as follows:

$$N_T = O_T \ x \ RF$$
$$N_T = 4.11 \ x \ 1.25$$
$$N_T = 5.14 \ \text{minutes}$$

The preceding paragraphs illustrate in capsule form the essential steps of rating a worker's observed speed.   Rating a person with precision requires a great deal of skill which can be acquired only through long years of practice and experience.   Most
industrial analysts attend special classes where they are taught how
to rate normal time.   They spend hours analyzing motion picture
films and conduct many time studies under close supervision.   In
view of the training that these analysts receive, it would be folly to
expect inexperienced library analysts to duplicate their consistency
or accuracy.   The best that can be expected is for the analyst to
exercise his best judgment, fully aware that his rating factor may
be in error by twenty-five per cent or more.

Adjusting Normal Time to Standard Time

If workers produced without interruption or break for eight straight hours, normal times could be used to calculate standard times. However, workers must be granted time off for personal needs, rest periods, and for events which are beyond their control. These adjustments are termed worker allowances and are added to normal time in order to produce a standard time for performing a job.

Barnes states that "for light work, where the operator works eight hours per day without rest periods, 2 to 5% (10 to 24 minutes) per day is all that the average worker will use for personal time."[3] This allowance time would appear to be appropriate for library studies. In most libraries, either officially or tacitly, workers are allowed personal time; but in addition, they are also allowed rest periods, which have become more or less synonymous with "coffee breaks." Usually an employee is allowed one break around mid-morning and another in mid-afternoon. Breaks seem to run anywhere from ten to twenty minutes each. Some people are still reluctant to accept the value of breaks, primarily because most library tasks do not involve physical exertion. However, studies tend to support the contention that a worker's output increases sharply immediately after a break, and that mental fatigue can produce the same effects on a worker as physical fatigue.

Delays may be either avoidable or unavoidable. Delays caused by the operator should be disregarded and not included in allowances. However, unavoidable delays must be considered. Two examples of unavoidable delays are machine break downs (charging machine, photo-reproduction equipment, etc.), or waiting for an elevator (e.g., vertical movement of book trucks in a multi-stack library). In order to ascertain reliably the amount of delay associated with a particular job, it is necessary to resort to all-day time study, or work sampling. Fortunately, most library oriented jobs do not involve much unavoidable delay time.

In order to illustrate how standard times are calculated, we can again refer to the binding preparation example. The library allows each employee two rest periods of twenty minutes each and twenty minutes personal time per eight-hour day. Delay time for the binding routine as observed is negligible and no allowance is made. The normal work day consists of 480 minutes (8 hours x 60 minutes/hour). Thus the total worker allowances are:

Personal needs allowance $= \dfrac{20}{480}$ minutes/day $= 4\%$

Fatigue allowance $= \dfrac{40}{480}$ minutes/day $= 8\%$

Delay allowance $= 0$

Percentage of total working day
permitted for allowances

$\overline{12\%}$

The standard time can now be computed by substitution into the following formula:

Standard time (S_T) = Normal time (N_T) x $\dfrac{100}{100 \text{ - Percentage of total working day permitted for allowances (A)}}$

$S_T = N_T$ x $\dfrac{100}{100 - A}$

$S_T = 5.14$ x $\dfrac{100}{100 - 12}$

$S_T = 5.84$

The standard time for the binding process is 5.84 minutes per volume prepared. Thus, if a worker devoted his entire day to this process, a supervisor could expect an output of 82 volumes (480/5.84 = 82).

A Method for Approximating Standard Times

The reason for converting observed times to standard times should be obvious. It should be equally obvious that the study technique itself introduces several types of errors. There will be timing errors, particularly if a regular watch is used for timing; rating errors are virtually assured -- the only question is their magnitude; and sampling will also introduce some errors. This seeming preoccupation with errors is not intended to belittle the value of time study, but to underscore that the results of time studies, particularly in libraries, will not be as precise as one might expect.

Fortunately, as mentioned previously, very few library studies require a high degree of precision. If for no other reason, job frequencies are not sufficiently great for tenths of seconds or seconds to become a critical factor. One method for approximating standard times is to add 50% to the observed times. For other time costs, and added non-time costs, please see Chapter X.

Notes

1. In a minority of cases, correction or retyping due to mistakes was necessary. This would be an example of an infrequent element. It is not shown here.

2. It should be noted that the entire process could and probably would be done in batches, pulling several specification cards at once, and so on. In this case, we would work with smaller elements in order to keep the individual timings relatively shorter.

3. Ralph M. Barnes, Motion and Time Study, Design and Measurement of Work, (New York, Wiley, 1963), p. 401.

Bibliography

General

Each of the two books listed below contains an extensive bibliography:

> Barnes, Ralph M. Motion and Time Study. 5th ed. New York: Wiley, 1963. Chapters 24-26.

> Mundel, Marvin E. Motion and Time Study. 3rd ed. Englewood Cliffs, N.J. : Prentice-Hall, 1960. Chapters 17-24.

Libraries

For up to 1954 consult:

> Logsden, Richard. "Time and Motion Studies in Libraries," Library Trends, II, No. 3 (January, 1954), p. 401-09.

For studies since 1954 look in Library Literature under the headings:

> Time and Motion Study and Time and Cost Studies.

Chapter VIII
Sampling

In making a management study the magnitude of the total group (universe) about which we wish to make generalizations frequently makes the examination of every member of the group prohibitively costly and time-consuming. To examine the total circulation record for a year in a library circulating 218,000 volumes per year (the circulation of the main library alone in the medium size public library system whose circulation system is described in Chapters XII and XIII) would be a herculean task. Fortunately, the examination of every member of the total group (in this case a "member" being the record of an individual circulation) is usually unnecessary because it is possible to select a relatively small number of the individual members and generalize from them with reasonable assurance that they are representative of the entire group. The picking out and analyzing of the members is known as sampling. The members selected are a sample.

Let us suppose that there was an urgent need to know the number of cards currently in the 1152 drawer (all of the drawers contain cards) North Carolina Union Catalog.

Counting all the cards (assuming we counted carefully) would provide an accurate answer. However, the time required to do this would be enormous. This work could be reduced to a small fraction of that required to count all the cards by using the following device: Since it is easy to ascertain the approximate number of cards per inch, it is possible to substitute the quicker method of measuring inches of cards. This figure can then be converted into numbers of cards by multiplying it by the number of cards per inch. But even to measure the cards in 1152 drawers, not to mention having to sum their measurements, would require considerable labor. Therefore, instead of counting all of the cards a sample will be drawn.

115

If all the drawers in the catalog contained the same number
of cards, the sample would need to consist of one drawer only.
We would merely measure the inches of cards in the drawer and
multiply this number by the number of cards per inch and by the
total number of drawers.   Since it is inevitable that some drawers
will contain more cards than others, the answer would be incorrect.   Therefore, several drawers, although still only a small fraction of the total must be included in the sample.   The number of
inches of cards in the individual drawers of the sample will be determined; this sum will then be multiplied by the number of cards
per inch and divided by the number of drawers in the sample.
This arithmetic will yield an average number of cards per drawer.
Finally, this figure will be multiplied by the number of drawers in
the catalog to yield the total number of cards in the catalog, which
is the information we need.   Let us decide arbitrarily to begin
with a trial sample of twenty drawers.

Random Selection of the Sample

The chief precaution to observe in picking a sample -- in
this case, 20 out of 1152 drawers -- is to make certain that the
members comprising it are chosen at random.   This means that it
is necessary to choose the members in such a way that the probability of choosing any one is the same as the probability of choosing any other.   In practice the most efficient way to choose a random sample is to use a table of random numbers.   Before turning
to a random number table, it will be necessary to assign numbers
to the total group.   The North Carolina Union Catalog drawers happen to be numbered (1-1152).   If they were not, it would be easy
to assign a number to each of them.   If the numbers must be assigned a quick sketch is a convenience.   This would enable quick
location of specific drawers when observations are being made.   If
we were dealing with a total group with no obvious geometric or
other pattern -- such as a group of books not circulated in the
past year or a group of users who had books overdue last January
-- the names would be recorded in any arbitrary manner and then
numbered consecutively.

Random Number Tables

A table of random numbers consists of digits arranged randomly in column and rows. Tables vary in length and arrangement. The table in this chapter (See Figure 8-1) contains 5,000 digits. Rand Corporation has produced a table of 1,000,000 digits. There is a table by Kendall and Smith of 100,000 digits. There are other printed tables of 41,600 digits (Tippett) and 15,000 digits (Fisher and Yates). The Bureau of Transport Economics and Statistics of the Interstate Commerce Commission produced, in 1940, a table of 105,000 digits. It is not easily available, but one will find excerpts from it in other books.

For any one sampling problem the table employed should be long enough to provide an adequate sample without using all of the numbers. The 100,000 digit table by Kendall and Smith is available for only $1.50.

Where to Begin in the Random Number Table

The next order of business is to determine where and how to begin in a random number table. One starts initially at the beginning of the table and reads straight through in any given direction. When the end of the table is reached, the user returns to the beginning and starts over again. Since a single use should not carry one all the way through the table, the point where the reading ended for any particular use should be carefully marked and the next subsequent reading begun at that point. Some individuals find it most convenient to read random tables down the column, probably because they are used to seeing numbers in columns in other contents. Others prefer to read across to the right, the same way a book is read. Unless the table stipulates otherwise the user should select whatever direction is most convenient to him and then be consistent about it.

Reading the Random number table to Obtain the Sample

Returning to the North Carolina Union Catalog example, let us now use Figure 1 of this chapter to pick the 20 drawer sample. The highest numbered drawer is 1152. Since this is a four digit number, we must read the table digits in groups of four. There

Random Sampling Numbers Produced by the Machine
1st Thousand

23157	54859	01837	25993	76249	70886	95230	36744
05545	55043	10537	43508	90611	83744	10962	21343
14871	60350	32404	36223	50051	00322	11543	80834
38976	74951	94051	75853	78805	90194	32428	71695
97312	61718	99755	30870	94251	25841	54882	10513
11742	69381	44339	30872	32797	33118	22647	06850
43361	28859	11016	45623	93009	00499	43640	74036
93806	20478	38268	04491	55751	18932	58475	52571
49540	13181	08429	84187	69538	29661	77738	09527
36768	72633	37948	21569	41959	68670	45274	83880
07092	52392	24627	12067	06558	45344	67338	45320
43310	01081	44863	80307	52555	16148	89742	94647
61570	06360	06173	63775	63148	95123	35017	46993
31352	83799	10779	18941	31579	76448	62584	86919
57048	86526	27795	93692	90529	56546	35065	32254
09243	44200	68721	07137	30729	75756	09298	27650
97957	35018	40894	88329	52230	82521	22532	61587
93732	59570	43781	98885	56671	66826	95996	44569
72621	11225	00922	68264	35666	59434	71687	58167
61020	74418	45371	20794	95917	37866	99536	19378
97839	85474	33055	91718	45473	54144	22034	23000
89160	97192	22232	90637	35055	45489	88438	16361
25966	88220	62871	79265	02823	52862	84919	54883
81443	31719	05049	54806	74690	07567	65017	16543
11322	54931	42362	34386	08624	97687	46245	23245

2nd Thousand

64755	83885	84122	25920	17696	15655	95045	95947
10302	52289	77436	34430	38112	49067	07348	23328
71017	98495	51308	50374	66591	02887	53765	69149
60012	55605	88410	34879	79655	90169	78800	03666
37330	94656	49161	42802	48274	54755	44553	65090
47869	87001	31591	12273	60626	12822	34691	61212
38040	42737	64167	89578	39323	49324	88434	38706
73508	30908	83054	80078	86669	30295	56460	45336
32623	46474	84061	04324	20628	37319	32356	43969
97591	99549	36630	35106	62069	92975	95320	57734
74012	31955	59790	96982	66224	24015	96749	07589
56754	26457	13351	05014	90966	33674	69096	33488
49800	49908	54831	21998	08528	26372	92923	65026
43584	89647	24878	56670	00221	50193	99591	62377
16653	79664	60325	71301	35742	83636	73058	87229
48502	69055	65322	58748	31446	80237	31252	96367
96765	54692	36316	86230	48296	38352	23816	64094
38923	61550	80357	81784	23444	12463	33992	28128
77958	81694	25225	05587	51073	01070	60218	61961
17928	28065	25586	08771	02641	85064	65796	48170
94036	85978	02318	04499	41054	10531	87431	21596
47460	60479	56230	48417	14372	85167	27558	00368
47856	56088	51992	82439	40644	17170	13463	18288
57616	34653	92298	62018	10375	76515	62986	90756
08300	92704	66752	66610	57188	79107	54222	22013

Fig. 8-1 A Table of 5,000 Random Digits

Reproduced from M. G. Kendall and B. B. Smith. "Randomness and Random Sampling Numbers," Journal of the Royal Statistical Society, 101 (1938), p. 147-66. By permission of the Royal Statistical Society and the authors.

3rd Thousand

89221	02362	65787	74733	51272	30213	92441	39651
04005	99818	63918	29032	94012	42363	01261	10650
98546	38066	50856	75045	40645	22841	53254	44125
41719	84401	59226	01314	54581	40398	49988	65579
28733	72489	00785	25843	24613	49797	85567	84471
65213	83927	77762	03086	80742	24395	68476	83792
65553	12678	90906	90466	43670	26217	69900	31205
05668	69080	73029	85746	58332	78231	45986	92998
39302	99718	49757	79519	27387	76373	47262	91612
64592	32254	45879	29431	38320	05981	18067	87137
07513	48792	47314	83660	68907	05336	82579	91582
86593	68501	56638	99800	82839	35148	56541	07232
83735	22599	97977	81248	36838	99560	32410	67614
08595	21826	54655	08204	87990	17033	56258	05384
41273	27149	44293	69458	16828	63962	15864	35431
00473	75908	56238	12242	72631	76314	47252	06347
86131	53789	81383	07868	89132	96182	07009	86432
33849	78359	08402	03586	03176	88663	08018	22546
61870	41657	07468	08612	98083	97349	20775	45091
43898	65923	25078	86129	78491	97653	91500	80786
29939	39123	04548	45985	60952	06641	28726	46473
38505	85555	14388	55077	18657	94887	67831	70819
31824	38431	67125	25511	72044	11562	53279	82268
91430	03767	13561	15597	06750	92552	02391	38753
38635	68976	25498	97526	96458	03805	04116	63514

4th Thousand

02490	54122	27944	39364	94239	72074	11679	54082
11967	36469	60627	83701	09253	30208	01385	37482
48256	83465	49699	24079	05403	35154	39613	03136
27246	73080	21481	23536	04881	89977	49484	93071
32532	77265	72430	70722	86529	18457	92657	10011
66757	98955	92375	93431	43204	55825	45443	69265
11266	34545	76505	97746	34668	26999	26742	97516
17872	39142	45561	80146	93137	48924	64257	59284
62561	30365	03408	14754	51798	08133	61010	97730
62796	30779	35497	70501	30105	08133	00997	91970
75510	21771	04339	33660	42757	62223	87565	48468
87439	01691	63517	26590	44437	07217	98706	39032
97742	02621	10748	78803	38337	65226	92149	59051
98811	06001	21571	02875	21828	83912	85188	61624
51264	01852	64607	92553	29004	26695	78583	62998
40239	93376	10419	68610	49120	02941	80035	99317
26936	59186	51667	27645	46329	44681	94190	66647
88502	11716	98299	40974	42394	62200	69094	81646
63499	38093	25593	61995	79867	80569	01023	38374
36379	81206	03317	78710	73828	31083	60509	44091
93801	22322	47479	57017	59334	30647	43061	26660
29856	87120	56311	50053	25365	81265	22414	02431
97720	87931	88265	13050	71017	15177	06957	92919
85237	09105	74601	46377	59938	15647	34177	92753
75746	75268	31727	95773	72364	87324	36879	06802

Fig. 8-1 A Table of 5,000 Random Digits

Reproduced from M. G. Kendall and B. B. Smith. "Randomness and Random Sampling Numbers," Journal of the Royal Statistical Society, 101 (1938), p. 147-66. By permission of the Royal Statistical Society and the authors.

5th Thousand

29935	06971	63175	52579	10478	89379	61428	21363
15114	07126	51890	77787	75510	13103	42942	48111
03870	43225	10589	87629	22039	94124	38127	65022
79390	39188	40756	45269	65959	20640	14284	22960
30035	06915	79196	54428	64819	52314	48721	81594
29039	99861	28759	79802	68531	39198	38137	24373
78196	08108	24107	49777	09599	43569	84820	94956
15847	85493	91442	91351	80130	73752	21539	10986
36614	62248	49194	97209	92587	92053	41021	80064
40549	54884	91465	43862	35541	44466	88894	74180
40878	08997	14286	09982	90308	78007	51587	16658
10229	49282	41173	31468	59455	18756	08908	06660
15918	76787	30624	25928	44124	25088	31137	71614
13403	18796	49909	94404	64979	41462	18155	98335
66523	94596	74908	90271	10009	98648	17640	68909
91665	36469	68343	17870	25975	04662	21272	50620
67415	87515	08207	73729	73201	57593	96917	69699
76527	96996	23724	33448	63392	32394	60887	90617
19815	47789	74348	17147	10954	34355	81194	54407
25592	53587	76384	72575	84347	68918	05739	57222
55902	45539	63646	31609	95999	82887	40666	66692
02470	58376	79794	22482	42423	96162	47491	17264
18630	53263	13319	97619	35859	12350	14632	87659
89673	38230	16063	92007	59503	38402	76450	33333
62986	67364	06595	17427	84623	14565	82860	57300

Fig. 8-1   A Table of 5,000 Random Digits

Reproduced from M. G. Kendall and B. B. Smith. "Randomness and Random Sampling Numbers," Journal of the Royal Statistical Society, 101 (1938), p. 147-66. By permission of the Royal Statistical Society and the authors.

are two basic rules to follow:

1. A number that is greater than the highest number that may be used must be skipped. Thus, in our example it will be necessary to ignore the numbers 1153-9999. Since the drawer numbering begins with 1, rather than with 0, it will also be necessary to ignore 0000.

2. A number that has already been selected for the sample should be ignored if it is drawn a second time.

Let us say that it is our habit to read the random table as a book, and that the last time we used it we stopped in the 2nd block of 1,000 digits, the 24th row from the top of the block, and the 38th column from the left (with a 7). Now, beginning with the 2nd block of 1,000 numbers, the 24th row from the top, and the 39th column from the left, we begin to read from left to right, starting with 56. Then, moving to the left end of the block and jumping down one row, as in reading a book, we read 08300 92704...... Starting then with 56 and reading groups of four digits, we get 5608 (which we must disregard), 3009 (which we must disregard), 2704 (which we must disregard), 1057 (which is the first member of the sample), and so on. For practice the reader should verify that the sample consists of the following drawers:

1.	1057	11.	0082
2.	0213	12.	1072
3.	0059	13.	0676
4.	0124	14.	0487
5.	0126	15.	0700
6.	1106	16.	0840
7.	0398	17.	0801
8.	0078	18.	0746
9.	0312	19.	0839
10.	0505	20.	0807

In actually recording the number of inches of cards in each sample drawer it is a convenience to have the drawers arranged on the recording sheet in numerical order. Therefore, in practice the sample numbers should not be recorded on a single sheet, as above, but rather on cards or slips, with one number per card.

These slips may then be sorted into numerical order. This procedure is also efficient for catching duplicate numbers. For every
duplicate caught, a replacement must be selected from the table.

When forced to bypass most of the numbers read (88.5% in
the example), reading the tables can, particularly for larger
samples, be tedious and time-consuming, and in any case is wasteful of table numbers. In such cases it is good practice, at least
if a desk calculator is handy, or if the number of items in the total group from which the sample is selected is one convenient for
mental division (such as 1000, 100, 50, 20, or the like), to adopt
an alternative procedure. The digits are grouped as the problem
requires and read consecutively. Each group of digits is divided
by the total number of items in the group from which the sample
is being selected. The remainder represents an item of the
sample. In our example the first four digit number read is 5608.
Dividing 5608 by 1152, one obtains a remainder of 1000. Drawer
number 1000 is then the first member of the sample drawn by this
method. The remainder zero represents the number 1152 itself.
Since 1152 does not divide evenly into 9999, all table numbers
above 9216 (1152 x 8) must be ignored, and also 0000, since the
drawer numbering begins with one. However, these numbers represent only 8% of the total possibilities -- as opposed to 88% using
the former method. The reader should verify that, using the division method of selection, the sample drawers would be:

1.	1000	11.	0237
2.	0705	12.	1058
3.	0400	13.	0058
4.	0915	14.	0818
5.	0362	15.	0835
6.	1057	16.	1047
7.	0735	17.	0419
8.	1043	18.	0213
9.	0814	19.	0028
10.	1068	20.	0244

Tables of Random Permutations

Tables of random permutations arrange a given group of integers in a random order. There are tables of a wide variety of range available: 0-9, 0-19, 1-9, 1-16, 1-20, 1-30, 1-50, 1-100, 1-200, 1-500, and even 1-1000. As of this writing, the authors know of no generally available random permutation table of more than 1000 numbers. Figure 8-2 is a sample random permutation for the numbers 1-500.

This variety of range can in some instances give a table of random permutations considerable advantage over a decimal table of random numbers for sample selection. Suppose that a sample of 20 card drawers is to be selected from a catalog with a total of 487 drawers. Using a random table, all numbers from 488 to 999 would have to be ignored (plus 000 if the drawer numbers begin with one) -- that is, an average of only 48% of the digits scanned could be used. If, however, the sample was selected by reading the 1-500 permutation of Figure 8-2, it would be necessary to ignore only 488-500 -- less than 3% of the numbers. A second advantage of random permutations is that, unlike the random number table, duplicate numbers have already been eliminated. As an example, let us use Figure 8-2 to select a sample of 20 from 487 drawer. Beginning at the upper left of the permutation and reading it the way a book is read, the sample is:

1.	428	11.	265
2.	083	12.	033
3.	293	13.	490
4.	004	14.	103
5.	234	15.	285
6.	200	16.	348
7.	257	17.	298
8.	397	18.	443
9.	095	19.	354
10.	114	20.	470

Of course the same random permutation cannot be used over and over for the same investigation. Therefore, several permutations of the same range are usually printed together. For example, the book from which Figure 8-2 was taken contains 38 different permutations of 1-500 and (because they require less space per permutation) 960 different permutations of 1-9.

The disadvantage of tables of random permutations is that as of this writing there are no tested tables of over 1-1000 range generally available. Therefore, in selecting a total group of over 1000 items -- such as the 1152 drawers of the major chapter example, they cannot be used.

428	83	293	4	234	200	257	397	95	114	265	33	490	103	285
348	298	443	354	470	158	195	223	401	168	391	431	127	336	104
320	39	387	66	496	101	86	380	242	304	46	37	495	295	414
18	68	375	485	185	343	34	25	358	361	384	402	416	92	125
188	15	473	308	474	16	197	24	329	106	243	54	198	80	28
186	349	79	203	72	413	85	56	107	75	418	425	347	394	269
475	386	253	263	437	193	180	423	405	244	389	251	487	2	43
11	351	286	306	333	235	214	325	146	468	218	376	82	138	50
381	178	464	162	274	29	372	364	362	196	270	453	73	71	399
481	445	155	328	324	133	340	23	262	211	241	139	282	315	140
228	160	471	489	260	318	478	165	88	484	472	494	232	250	290
74	153	287	115	254	97	49	132	365	486	310	497	432	393	61
151	458	457	120	322	187	404	137	346	216	499	51	63	182	176
360	411	449	396	410	240	117	281	32	313	118	412	271	488	247
479	10	350	332	126	76	229	296	128	385	99	174	109	288	335
290	119	239	466	424	237	129	398	209	148	94	3	102	316	463
319	433	444	477	121	47	379	202	27	435	179	238	8	98	113
278	201	400	45	420	167	382	170	338	144	455	221	122	52	317
42	231	450	173	305	206	280	35	123	141	419	339	236	78	7
273	110	112	258	36	307	447	210	177	58	341	246	96	233	374
192	314	355	84	89	227	476	326	377	448	483	134	323	283	469
456	249	26	184	108	311	275	276	53	408	367	40	330	220	226
44	20	116	145	67	373	465	164	152	194	131	59	267	157	438
87	199	446	462	142	207	149	409	301	427	452	388	421	368	224
294	30	345	69	136	369	344	417	111	261	439	366	1	91	166
135	81	363	454	392	292	6	383	159	147	422	225	124	21	64
38	434	334	70	65	156	353	105	171	217	451	93	337	31	492
17	300	191	259	321	467	430	252	77	248	13	331	352	429	441
491	327	500	143	407	245	302	266	459	181	268	297	371	461	183
436	299	460	312	272	5	498	219	215	163	493	356	205	172	357
426	62	169	14	303	370	100	55	48	378	279	130	60	440	277
406	291	222	403	395	255	342	57	264	415	212	19	256	230	12
213	390	161	9	190	154	90	150	175	309	284	359	204	22	208
482	41	189	442	480										

Fig. 8-2　A random permutation of the integers 1-500

Reproduced by permission of Stanford University Press from: L. E. Moses and R. Oakford, Tables of Random Permutations (California: Stanford University Press, 1963), p. 174.

Determining the Required Sample Size

In the North Carolina Union Catalog example we arbitrarily chose a sample size of 20 card drawers out of a total group of 1152 drawers. Is this sample size sufficient to furnish a reliable average of the inches of cards per drawer? Or do we need to sample 50 drawers or even 100 drawers to obtain an accurate answer? It is obvious that in both this type of problem and in time study problems (where the observations are units of time rather than units of cards) this is a crucial matter. The purpose of the next few sections of this chapter is to show how to answer this question.

Deciding on the Sample Reliability Required

The closer to 100% certainty that an investigator demands that his sample approach, the larger it will have to be. He must therefore begin by making two decisions as to how reliable an answer he needs or desires.

The most common practice is to use a 95% confidence level. This means that the sampler can be confident that his random observations will represent the facts 95% of the time. It also means that 5% of the time they will not. However, these are good odds. Since practicing management people find them satisfactory for most of their purposes, it is recommended that these guidelines also be adopted for library studies. The next most common confidence level is 99%. Since a 99% confidence level is seldom necessary in management practice, and since the 4% increase in certainty may require a substantial increase in sample size, it is recommended that it be used sparingly.

The second decision is with regard to the sample average. This average is obtained by summing the values of the observations and then dividing by the number of observations. In statistics this average is usually called the arithmetic mean and is designated by the symbol $\overline{X}$ (X-bar). In any sample the sample average is expected to vary somewhat from the true average of the total group from which the sample was taken. This variation is expressed in terms of percentage, which is then converted into a range of val-

ues. As an illustration, let us use $\pm 5\%$ variation and suppose
that upon sampling the 20 card drawers, we obtained an average of
722 cards per drawer. We multiply 722 by 5%: 722 x 0.05 =   36.
The true average of the group then lies somewhere between 722
minus 36 and 722 plus 36 -- i. e. , between 686 and 758.   The
smaller the per cent of variation allowed -- i. e. , the closer to the
true average of the group that we insist our average sample be --
the larger our sample will have to be.   The most common practice
is to insist on a variation of no more than $\pm 5\%$, and it is recommended that this figure be adopted as a guideline for library studies.

To combine the decision of 95% confidence with that of
$\pm 5\%$ variation means that the sampler can be 95% sure and that
his sample average is not more than 5% above or less than 5% below the true average of the total group from which the sample was
taken.

The Required Sample Size Formula

Once the confidence and variation decisions are made, it is
possible to develop a specific formula to show when the sample is
large enough to meet these requirements.   Although the formula
for any given set of decisions is developed in the same general
manner, its constant value will vary with each different set.   Only
the formula for 95% confidence and $\pm 5\%$ variation will be discussed in this text.   By studying the formula's derivation (See the
chapter bibliography) the interested reader will learn how to construct comparable formulas for any other set of decision values.

The working formula for 95% confidence and $\pm 5\%$ variation
is:

$$N' = \frac{1600 \left[N\Sigma X^2 - (\Sigma X)^2 \right]}{(\Sigma X)^2}$$

N' = the number of observations needed to meet the criteria
     of 95% conficence and $\pm 5\%$ variation

N = the number of observations actually taken

ΣX = the sum of the value of all the observations

$(\Sigma X)^2$ = the square of the sum of the values of all of the observations, i. e. , ΣX multiplied by itself.

ΣX^2 = the sum of the squares of the values of all the observations

and 1600 is the square of the constant used at this confidence level.

Recording the Observations

The observations should be recorded in a form convenient for calculation. There should be space for the X^2 values adjacent to the X values. If the Xs and X^2s are to be added mentally, most persons will find it convenient to record them in columns rather than rows, and with the decimal points in line. The space allowed for recording should be appropriate to the magnitude of the numbers being recorded. Lined paper, graph paper, accounting paper or a homemade form such as is shown in Figure 8-3 will help to keep the work orderly and manageable. The observation sheet should bear all pertinent information about the sampling: Where it was done, When, By whom, and the units in which the observations are recorded. The first 20 observations (the trial sample) of the North Carolina Union Catalog are recorded in Figure 8-3 as observations 1-20.

Determining if Additional Observations Are Necessary

We now have the required data to substitute into and solve the above formula:

(1)
$$N' = \frac{1600 \left[N\Sigma X^2 - (\Sigma X)^2 \right]}{(\Sigma X)^2}$$

(2)
$$N' = \frac{1600 \left[20(1320.51) - (161.3)^2 \right]}{(161.3)^2}$$

(3)
$$N' = \frac{1600(392.51)}{26017.69}$$

(4)
$$N' = \frac{628016.00}{26017.69}$$

(5)
$$N' = 24 \text{ observations}$$

	Observation Work Sheet									
Units Sampled: Inches of cards/drawer							Name: J. Smith			
Location: North Carolina Union Catalog, UNC Library.							Date: 9/1/1966			
Obs no.	Item selected	x	x²	Obs no.	Item selected	x	x²	Obs no.	Item selected	x	x²
1	0059	9.0	81.00	15	0807	8.0	64.00	27	0411	5.8	33.64
2	0078	9.5	90.25	16	0839	8.4	70.56	28	0441	7.9	62.41
3	0082	8.9	79.21	17	0840	7.8	60.48	29	0454	8.3	68.89
4	0124	9.1	82.81	18	1057	5.5	30.25	30	0707	8.4	70.56
5	0126	8.8	77.44	19	1072	7.4	54.76	Total		240.5	1961.75
6	0213	8.1	65.61	20	1106	8.1	65.61				
7	0312	8.3	68.89	Total		161.3	1320.51				
8	0398	7.5	56.25	1-20		161.3	1320.51				
9	0487	7.6	57.76	21	0109	9.2	84.64				
10	0505	8.5	72.25	22	0138	9.8	96.04				
11	0676	8.5	72.25	23	0208	8.9	79.21				
12	0700	7.8	60.84	24	0239	6.6	43.56				
13	0746	5.7	32.49	25	0340	7.3	53.29				
14	0801	8.8	77.44	26	0365	7.0	49.00				

Fig. 8-3   Sample observation work sheet.

For those readers who prefer to avoid equations, the form illustrated in Figure 8-4 was developed as an aid for the quick solution of the computational form of the sample size equation (See Figure 8-4).

The solution for the 20 drawer sample is recorded in the column headed: Observations 1-20. An explanation of the form is given below:

Step 1.   First, the values must be computed for the x^2 column of our observation sheet (See Figure 8-3). In some cases the answer will be known immediately e. g., $(8.0)^2 = 64.0$. In other cases it will not. It is recommended that the squares that cannot be worked mentally be obtained from a table. One common-

Step	Item	Observations 1-20	Observations 20-30	Observations
1.	Σx^2	1320.51	1961.75	
2.	N	20	30	
3.	$N\Sigma x^2$	26410.20	58852.50	
4.	$(\Sigma x)^2$	26017.69	57840.25	
5.	$N\Sigma x^2 - (\Sigma x)^2$	392.51	1012.25	
6.	$[N\Sigma x^2 - (\Sigma x)^2]$ x $1600/(\Sigma x)^2$	24	28	

Fig. 8-4 Determining the required sample size for
the North Carolina Union Catalog Sample.

ly available table (Barlow's) gives square of numbers up to 12,500
and there are many tables giving squares of numbers up to 1000
(See the chapter bibliography). Secondly, the x^2 values are added
which give Σx^2. This is the value recorded on the form.

Step 2. N is the number of observations.

Step 3. This value is the product of Σx^2 and N.

Step 4. First add the X column on the observation sheet
(Figure 8-3) to obtain ΣX. Then look up the square of this value
in a table. For convenience of subtraction, the $(\Sigma X)^2$ digits
should be lined up directly under the $N\Sigma x^2$ digits.

Step 5. This value is the remainder of $N\Sigma x^2 - (\Sigma X)^2$.

Step 6. This expression is solved quickly on the slide rule.
How to do this is described in the section of this book explaining
the slide rule (See Chapter IX). A desk calculator may be used if
one is handy. The answer is N', the number of observations required.

For the North Carolina Union Catalog sample, we need 24
observations, or 4 more than the 20 we have taken.

Making the Additional Observations

The formula indicates that four additional observations will
be required. However, the formula cannot predict the exact varia-

tion among these additional observations. If this variation happens
to be somewhat greater than that among the observations already
made, then, with such a small sample, a few more observations
will be needed than stated by the formula. To be on the safe side
we shall therefore make ten additional observations.

The last digit of the 20th observation was taken from the 3rd
group of 1000 digits, row 19, column 37 of the random table in
this book. Therefore, we begin to read the table for observations
21-30 with the 3rd 1000 digits, row 19, and column 38. We continue as before to read the table as a book. The reader should
verify that the following drawer numbers are selected:

21.	0454	26.	0208
22.	0441	27.	0138
23.	0239	28.	0707
24.	0411	29.	0365
25.	0109	30.	0340

The X, ΣX, X^2 and ΣX^2 values of these observations are recorded in Figure 8-3. From the cumulative data of observations
1-30 the required sample size (28) is computed using the procedure
outlined in Figure 8-4. We conclude that the 30 observations are
sufficient for 95% confidence and $\pm 5\%$ variation, and the problem
can now be completed. Since 30 drawers contain 240.5 inches of
cards, the average number of cards per drawer for the sample is
240.5/30, or 8.017 inches. If this average is within $\pm 5\%$ of the
true average for the catalog as a whole, then (since 8.017 x 0.05
= 0.401):

8.017 inches $+ 0.401$ inches = 8.418 inches of cards per drawer

8.017 inches $- 0.401$ inches = 7.616 inches of cards per drawer

The possible range of the average is then from 7.616 inches to
8.418 inches. At 90 cards per inch, we then determine the total
number of cards in the catalog as follows. Somewhere between:
8.418 inches of cards per drawer x 1152 drawers x 90 cards per
inch = 872,778 total cards; and 7.616 inches of cards per drawer
x 1152 drawers x 90 cards per inch = 789,627 total cards. This
answer will be quite accurate enough for most management purposes.

The reader who has been struggling along with ideas new to him may at this point be inclined to feel that sampling is more trouble than it is worth. A comparison of the approximate times involved with and without sampling for the North Carolina Union Catalog example shows clearly that this is not so. For the sampling technique.

1. Selecting the 20 item sample from
   the random number table   15 minutes

2. Arranging the sample drawer
   numbers in order   05 minutes

3. Making and recording the observations   15 minutes

4. Making all additions, calculations for
   sample size formula (incl. checking)   15 minutes

5. Selecting and arranging 10 more sample
   drawers from the random number table   10 minutes

6. Making and recording these 10 additional observations   10 minutes

7. Reworking the sample size formula   10 minutes

                              Total   1 hr. 20 min.

Now suppose that the sampling technique had been rejected and instead we decided to measure all the drawers. Since there are 1152 drawers, and making and recording the observations averaged about 3/4 minute per drawer, the work would take about 3/4 x 1152 minutes, or 14-plus hours, not to mention the tediousness of this type of work. This time does not, of course, include summing the 1152 individual drawer totals.

Either-or Sampling

So far this chapter has dealt only with quantities that can be arranged among themselves in an order of magnitude-- one card drawer contains more or fewer inches of cards than another drawer. However, it sometimes becomes necessary to draw samples from universes that can only be classified in terms of either-or. The cataloger either is or is not at his desk. The book either is or is not returned on time. The patron either uses or does not use the card catalog. The book a student borrows is either fiction or non-fiction. And so on. In these cases it would be nonsensical to say that one category is greater or less than another in the sense that 3 is greater than 2 but less than 4.

Although this sort of sampling has a variety of applications, its most frequent management use is in work sampling. Work sampling in turn has a variety of uses. One frequent application is the determination of the amount of time per day that an employee is idle or productive. Work sampling can also be used to distinguish different categories of productive work such as typing, filing, stamping, and shelving. The exact times during the day when an employee will be observed are determined by some random process. A random number table is commonly used. Each observation is then recorded simply as a mark under "idle" or "working." (One can of course add other categories if he desires more detailed information.) Just as with sampling quantities with magnitude, the number of observations required for either-or sampling will vary as with the fluctuations in the data, and the confidence level and average variation limits imposed by the analyst. For a confidence level of 95% and $\pm 5\%$ allowable variation, the computational form of the sample size formula (easily solved on the slide rule) is:

$$N' = \frac{1600\ (1-P)}{P}$$

where

    N' = the number of observations required

    P = the fraction: number of occurrences of the activity or delay being measured/total number of observations. It may be expressed as either a decimal or fraction -- use whichever is most convenient in a specific instance

The final answer may be simply the percentage of the total working day or week an employee or department is idle or productive. Or (for the moment associating P with idle, rather than productive, time), it is possible to convert these percentages into time idle or productive by the formulas:

    Hours idle per week = Hours per week on Job x P

    Hours productive per week = Hours per week on job x (1-P)

As an example, suppose that the librarian of a sizeable library wants to know the feasibility of utilizing part of the time at the circulation area in other departments of the library at non-peak

hours. If there are several employees in circulation, work sampling would be an efficient means of answering this question, for a
simultaneous sampling of all of the workers could be made by a
single observer. In contrast, a continuous time study, in addition
to being more burdensome, would require additional observers --
perhaps even one observer for each employee. The work sampling
study may ascertain that some employees are much more idle than
others. This may be no fault of the workers, but rather point to
poor supervision or poor work procedures or both. The study
could also be designed so that the analyst also kept a record of
what each individual was doing each time he was observed in order
to learn how the circulation people spend their time.

Bibliography

Random Number Tables

Barnes, Ralph M. Work Sampling. 2nd ed. New York: Wiley,
1957.

Contains a 17,500 digit extract from the 1949 table of ICC's
Bureau of Transport Economics and Statistics.

Fisher, Ronald, and Yates, Frank. Statistical Tables for Biologi-
cal, Agricultural, and Medical Research. 6th ed. rev.
and enl. New York: Hafner, 1963.

Table XXXIII consists of 7500 two-figure random numbers
arranged on six pages. Includes an introduction describing
some useful labor-saving devices.

Handbook of Mathematical Tables. 2nd ed. Supplement to Handbook of Chemistry and Physics. Cleveland: The Chemical Rubber Co., 1964.

Contains a 14,000 digit extract from the 1949 table of the
ICC's Bureau of Transport Economics and Statistics.

Interstate Commerce Commission. Bureau of Transport Economics
and Statistics. Table of 105,000 Random Decimal Digits.
Washington, D C., 1949.

Does not seem to be generally available. Not a depository
item. It has been identified as Bureau Statement no. 4914,
File no. 261-A-1. Rows and columns are spaced in groups
of five.

Kendall, Maurice G., and Smith, Babington B. "Randomness and
Random Sampling Numbers," Journal of the Royal Statistical
Society, CI (1938), p. 147-66.

The table of 5,000 random digits in this chapter was originally printed on pages 164-66.

----, ----, ----. Tables of Random Sampling Numbers. Cambridge: Cambridge University Press, 1946. (Tracts for
Computers, no. 24).

One-hundred thousand random digits. Broken into groups
of 1,000. Each 1,000 digits are arranged into 25 numbered
rows and 10 column groupings of four digits each. The
best random table buy around.

Rand Corporation. A Million Random Digits with 100,000 Normal
Deviates. Glencoe, Ill.: Free Press, 1955.

A fine table, but a stiff price of $17.50. Twenty-thousand
numbered rows; fifty rows and fifty columns per page.
Spacing is by fives.

Tippett, L. H. C. ...Random Sampling Numbers. Cambridge:
Cambridge University Press, 1927. (Tracts for computers,
no. 15).

Forty-one-thousand-six-hundred digits with the columns
spaced in fours and the rows in fives. A tried and true
table, and an excellent buy.

Tables of Random Permutations

Cochran, William G., and Cox, Gertrude M. Experimental De-
signs. 2nd ed. New York: Wiley, 1957.

Chapter 15 contains 1,000 random permutations of 9 numbers
and 800 permutations of 16 numbers. Also found in the
first edition, 1950.

Fisher, Ronald A., and Yates, Frank. Statistical Tables for Bio-
logical, Agricultural, and Medical Research. 6th ed. rev.
and enl. New York: Hafner, 1963.

Table XXXIII1 gives 750 random permutations numbered 0-
749 of the numbers 0-9. Table XXXIII2 gives 200 similar
permutations of the numbers 0-19. Also includes a helpful
introduction to the tables.

Moses, Lincoln E., and Oakford, Robert. Tables of Random Permutations. Standard: Stanford University Press, 1963.

Contains permutations of 9, 16, 20, 30, 50, 100, 200, 500 and
1,000 integers. The best tables available as of this writing.

The Sample Size Formula

Barnes, Ralph M. Motion and Time Study. 5th ed. New York:
Wiley, 1963. p. 365-8.

Mundel, Marvin E. Motion and Time Study. 3rd ed. Englewood
Cliffs, N. J.: Prentice-Hall, 1960. p. 363-68.

Tables of Squares

Barlow's Tables of Squares, Cubes, Square Roots, Cube Roots and
Reciprocals of all Integers up to 12,500.   4th ed.   New
York: Chemical Publishing Co. , 1954.

The most useful such compilation because of its great range.
There are many tables giving squares of integers 1-1000.
One will be found in any edition of the Handbook of Chemistry and Physics, or in practically any other general collection of mathematical tables.   Such tables are also found often in the back of statistics texts.

Work Sampling

Barnes, Ralph M.   Work Sampling.   2nd ed.   New York: Wiley,
1957.

A substantial portion of this material may be found also in
Barnes.   Motion and Time Study.   5th ed.   Chapter 33.

Hansen, Bertrand L.   Work Sampling for Modern Management.
Englewood Cliffs, N. J. :   Prentice-Hall, 1960.

Heiland, Robert E. , and Richardson, Wallace J.   Work Sampling.
New York: McGraw-Hill, 1957.

Poage, Scott T.   'Work Sampling in Library Administration.'   Library Quarterly, XXX, No. 3 (July, 1960), p. 213-18.

Sampling

Slonim, Morris J.   Sampling in a Nutshell.   New York: Simon
and Schuster, 1960.

A non-mathematical approach.

Sampling is a part of the broader subject of statistics.   Elementary
sampling is therefore covered in beginning books on statistics, of
which there are dozens in print.   Two standard ones are:

Franzblau, Abraham N.   A Primer of Statistics for Non-
Statisticians.   New York: Harcourt, 1958.

Moroney, M. J.   Facts from Figures.   3rd and rev. ed.
Harmondsworth, Middlesex, Penguin Books, 1956.

Chapter IX
Aids to Computation

Scientific management often involves simple arithmetic computation -- addition, subtraction, multiplication and division. This chapter describes some readily available tools and techniques that will help to keep the time and effort of these computations to a minimum and their accuracy to a maximum. The reader is urged to give each aid a fair trial. It is not a management virtue to do sloppy work or to do things the long, hard way. Fortunately, it is not necessary to do either.

Rounding Answers

In carrying out computations, one should carry along a couple of extra figures and then round back to the answer. The number of figures to retain in the answer depends on the particular situation. It would be foolish, for example, to say that 12.75 or even 12.7 observations are needed to make a valid sample. On the other hand, to say that there is an average of 12.7 or even 12.75 inches of cards per drawer in a catalog, if a ruler capable of measuring accurately to tenths and hundredths of an inch has been used, is not at all out of place. The principle to keep in mind is that an answer can be no more accurate than the data with which one has to work.

The common rules for rounding are:

If the digit next following (to the right of) the last place to be retained in the answer is:

1. Less than 5 leave the digit in the last place of the answer as it stands. Thus 12.0, 12.1, 12.2, 12.3, 12.4 are rounded to the nearest whole number = 12.

2. More than 5 add 1 to the digit in the last place of the answer. Thus 12.6, 12.7, 12.8, 12.9 are rounded to the nearest whole number = 13.

3. Exactly 5 look at the digit preceding (to the left of) it
-- i.e., look at the digit in the last place of the answer which one
wishes to retain:

A. If this preceding number is <u>even</u>, leave it as is in the
answer. Thus, 12.5 rounded to the nearest whole number is 12.

B. If this preceding number is <u>odd</u>, then add 1 to it in the
answer. Thus 11.5 rounded to the nearest whole number is 12.

Checking Arithmetic

If a management study is based upon arithmetical calculations, and management decisions will be based upon the results of
the study, it is important that the computations be correct, and
they should always be checked. The following checks are both
simple and fast. They are strongly recommended.

Addition

The usual method of checking addition in the U.S. is to re-
add the columns in the opposite direction from the original adding.
The logic behind this check is that by doing over the work in a reverse direction, a different sequence of numbers is added, which
makes it unlikely that a mistake will be repeated. This check is
effective, but for addition involving several rows of large numbers,
it is tedious.

There is an alternative check, commonly used in Europe,
which for practical purposes is just as accurate as the reverse-add
check and for large sums much less time-consuming. This technique is known as <u>casting out nines</u>. The method is shown in the
following illustration:

$
\begin{array}{llllll}
244.17 & 2 + 4 + 4 + 1 + 7 = 18; & 1 + 8 = 9; & 9 - 9 = 0 \\
982.90 & 9 + 8 + 2 + 9 + 0 = 28; & 2 + 8 = 10; & 1 + 0 = 1 \\
617.05 & 6 + 1 + 7 + 0 + 5 = 19; & 1 + 9 = 10; & 1 + 0 = 1 \\
488.25 & 4 + 8 + 8 + 3 + 5 = 27; & 2 + 7 = 9; & 9 - 9 = 0 \\
\hline
2332.37 & 2 + 3 + 3 + 2 + 3 + 7 = 20; & 2 + 0 = 2 & \overline{2}
\end{array}
$

The steps to be followed are:

A.   Add the digits in each row, including the sum-row:

    1. If the sum of the row is <u>less than 9,</u> that row is finished.

    2. If the sum of the row is exactly 9, "cast it out," leaving a
       row-sum of <u>0</u>.

3. If the sum of the row is <u>greater than</u> 9, then add its digits:

    A. If this sum is <u>less than</u> 9 that row is finished.

    B. If this sum is <u>exactly</u> 9, "cast it out," leaving a row-sum of <u>0</u>. (In casting out nines, the reduced-sum of a two digit number cannot exceed 9).

B. Add the final digits resulting from (A) for all rows except the sum-row (in the example, 0+1+1+0+ = 2). If the total is greater than 9, reduce it to a single digit as described in (A).

C. If the final digit resulting from (B) equals the final digit obtained by adding and reducing the sum-row in (A), then the addition is correct. If not, a mistake has been made. (In the example, both final digits are 2, so the addition is correct.)

The reader will learn quickly to pick out nines and combinations of digits that total nine and cast them out mentally, writing down only the final digit for each row. Thus, in actual practice, once the principle is mastered, the cross-check would look as shown below, and the actual check would not take more than a few seconds:

```
$   244. 17  0
    982. 90  1
    617. 05  1
    488. 25  0  = 2
  $ 2332. 37     2
```

Subtraction

Subtaction may also be checked by casting out nines, but it has no advantage over the common American check on subtraction, as indicated below:

Subtraction		Check	
$2332. 37	Minuend	$1993. 46	Subtrahend
- 1993. 46	Subtahend	+ 338. 91	Remainder
$ 338. 91	Remainder	$2332. 37	Minuend

In practice the check would not be written out at all, for it may be done mentally merely by adding "up." Thus in the example we think:

1+6 = 7, 9+4 = 13, 9+3 = 12, 4+9 = 13, 4=   4+9 = 13, 1+1 =2.

Multiplication

Casting out nines is by far the simplest way to check multi-plication.   The standard American method is to remultiply in the reverse order.   Thus, for example:

Original multiplication	Check
$347. 23	$982. 16
x 982. 16	x347. 23
208338	294648
34723	196432
69446	687512
277784	392864
312507	294648
$341035. 4168	$341035. 4168

In contrast, the casting out nines check is:

Multiplicand $347. 23   1
Multiplier   x 982. 16   x8
                  $341035. 4168   8

(cross diagram: 1 at top, 8 left, 8 right, 8 bottom)

The steps are as follows:

1. The multiplicand, multiplier, and product rows are added just as in the addition example, casting out nines until the sum of each row has been reduced to a single digit.   (In the example, $3+4+7+2+3 = 19$; the 9 is cast out leaving 1).

2. The multiplicand digit is multiplied by the multiplier dig-it and the product is recorded.   (In the example, $1 \times 8 = 8$).   If the product happens to be a two digit number, it is reduced in the usual way to a single digit.

3. The sum of the product row should be equal to the prod-uct of step 2.   If it is not, the multiplication is incorrect.   (In the example, $8 = 8$, so the answer is correct).

It is customary and convenient, although certainly not neces-sary, to record this check in the form of a cross, as shown at the right of the example.   The upper quarter is for the sum of the multiplicand row, the lower quarter for the sum of the multiplier row, and the right quarter for the product of these two digits.   The left quarter is for the sum of the product row.

Division

Casting out nines is also by far the simplest way to check division.   The standard method is by multiplication and addition.

The formula is:

$$\text{Dividend} = (\text{Divisor} \times \text{Quotient}) + \text{Remainder}$$

A division problem has been worked out below at the left. The long check is given to its immediate right. The casting out nines check is to the far right. It parallels the long check exactly. The only difference is that casting out reduces the dividend, divisor, quotient, and remainder to single digits so that the multiplication and addition may be performed mentally:

Division	Long Check	Casting Out Nines

```
        1 99.        14. 68  Divisor  1
14. 68 )2935. 17     x 199   Quotient x1
        1468         13212
        14671        13212
        13212        1468
        14597        2921. 32  Product    1
        13212        - 13. 85  Remainder +8
        1385         2935. 17  Dividend    0
```

Casting Out Nines diagram:
1
0 / 1+ 8 = 0
1
=
Divisor, Dividend, Product + Remainder, Quotient

Two Special Rulers Useful in Management Work

Engineer's Ruler

The engineer's ruler is an everyday tool in civil engineering, map drawing, and graphic layout. It is made of boxwood or plastic, and may be either triangular or flat. The triangular version carries six different scales -- one on each side of each edge. These scales commonly have 10, 20, 30, 40, 50 and 60 graduations per inch and are accordingly designated on the rule by a 10, 20, 30, 40, 50, or 60. Figure 9-1 shows an engineer's scale which is flat in cross section. It carries four scales -- a 10 and 40 on the side pictured and a 30 (or 20) and 50 on the reverse.

One practical illustration of library application is the measurement of the inches of cards in the catalog in the sampling chapter example. Since the cards were measured to the nearest 1/10 inch, the 10 scale was used. For more accurate measurement the 50 scale (each graduation representing 2/100 inch) would be used. An ordinary ruler, which divides the inch into 16th and 32nds, would have yielded fractions less convenient for computation, while the engineer's ruler enables retention of the familiar inch unit

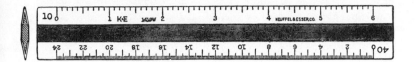

Fig. 9-1 Engineer's Ruler

without inconvenience in computation.

Another example of application is for forms design. In the chapter on forms, it was pointed out that the width of each space is normally measured in tenths of an inch (10 scale). Spacing between the lines varies among the following possibilities:

1/3 inch (10 graduations on the 30 scale or 20 graduations on the 60 scale)

1/4 inch (5 graduations on the 20 scale or 10 graduations on the 40 scale)

1/5 inch (2 graduations on the 10 scale or 10 graduations on the 50 scale)

1/6 inch (5 graduations on the 30 scale or 10 graduations on the 60 scale)

Thus, in contrast to using an ordinary ruler, by using an engineer's ruler one is able to make all of these different measurements conveniently and precisely with no estimation between graduations necessary.

The engineer's ruler may also be used for drawing and measuring scale diagrams of appropriate reduction (as 1/2 size, 1/3 size, etc.) in the same manner as the architect's rule, which is described next following. This use is not emphasized here for the reason that most scale drawings a librarian will have to contend with are of buildings and building layouts, and the scales of the architect's ruler are usually more convenient for this purpose.

Architect's Ruler

The architect's ruler is an everyday tool in architectural drawing and mechanical and electrical engineering. Like the engi-

neer's ruler, it is made of boxwood or plastic and may be either
triangular or flat.   The triangular version usually carries eleven
different scales.   One side of one scale carries a twelve inch
scale divided into 16ths of an inch and is designated by a 16.   The
remaining five edge-sides carry two scales each.   These scales
are graduated in twelfths or fractions thereof for lengths of 3
inches down to 3/32 inches and are designated accordingly as 3...
3/32.   Figure 9-2 shows an architect's ruler which is flat.   It carries eight scales -- 1, 1/2, 1/4, 1/8 on the side pictured, and
3/8, 3/4, 1 1/2, and 3 on the reverse.

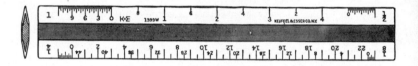

Courtesy of Keuffel & Esser Co.
Fig. 9-2 Architect's Ruler

The Slide Rule

So far as the librarian needs be concerned, the slide rule
is a device which allows him to perform multiplication and division
much more rapidly and easily than could be done by hand.   The
one limitation is that the product or quotient will be accurate to only three significant figures (or we might possibly miss the third
figure by 1).   This is quite accurate enough for a wide variety of
management applications, and in any case, the slide rule serves as
a check on other computations.   Thus the small amount of time
and effort necessary to master slide rule multiplication and division
is a sound management investment.

Varieties of Slide Rules

Slide rules are made in various shapes and sizes.   The one
in general use is in the shape of a ruler (See Figure 9-3).   It has
a central sliding part and a glass runner or indicator which may be
slid up and down the face of the ruler.   The indicator is bisected

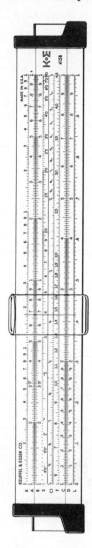

Courtesy Keuffel & Es-
ser Co.
Fig. 9-3 A Slide Rule

laterally by a hairline.   The most common
size rule has 10'' long scales.   The scales
are of different sorts and are identified by
letters of the alphabet.   Some rules have
more scales than others.   However, the
reader need not be concerned about this for,
whatever the variety, the rule will always
have a C and a D scale, and these are the
only two required for multiplication and division.   There are many different grades of
slide rule manufactured.   The cost of a 10''
slide rule may range anywhere from $2.00
to $25.00 or more.   Whatever the quality of
the rule the reader chooses to learn on, it
should be the standard 10'' size rather than
one of the smaller varieties.

Number Division on the C and D Scales

Understanding the number divisions on
the C and D scales is the key to facility with
the slide rule.   Since the two scales are
identical, to learn one is to learn both.

Locate the scales.   The D scale is on
the stationary part of the rule and the C
scale is adjacent to it on the central sliding
part.

The C and D scales have primary,
secondary, and tertiary divisions which are
associated respectively with the first, second,
and third figures of the numbers that are being multiplied or divided.

There are nine primary divisions of
unequal length.   The boundaries of these divisions are indicated by the large numerals
1, 2, 3, 4, 5, 6, 7, 8, 9, 1, (See Figure 9-4).   The
left hand 1 is called the left index and the

right hand 1, the <u>right index</u>. The primary divisions decrease in length as one reads across the scale from left to right. Thus the distance between 1 and 2 is greater than that between 2 and 3; the distances between 2 and 3 greater than that between 3 and 4; and so on.

Courtesy of Keuffel & Esser Co.
Fig. 9-4

There are three different sorts of secondary and tertiary divisions, each associated with a different section of the C and D scale: Section one runs from the left index to primary division 2; section two from primary division 2 to primary division 4; and section three from primary division 4 to the right index.

Section one: left index -- Primary division 2 (See Figure 9-5):

Courtesy of Keuffel & Esser Co.
Fig. 9-5

There are ten secondary divisions. The boundaries are indicated, left to right, by the left index, (small) 1, 2, 3, 4, 5, 6, 7, 8, 9, (large 2). The space between each secondary division is also divided into tenths. Thus the scale between the left index and 2 is subdivided into 10 x 10 or 100 subparts, and each tertiary division has a value of 1. We can accordingly read three significant figures exactly but must estimate the fourth figure.

Section two: Primary Division 2 -- Primary division 4 (See Figure 9-6):

There are ten unnumbered secondary divisions between 2 and 3 and between 3 and 4. However, each secondary division is divided into fifths, rather than tenths as in section one. Thus there are only 10 x 5 or 50 divisions between 2 and 3 and between

3 and 4, and each tertiary division has a value of two. If the third significant figure is even, we may set it exactly. If it is odd, we estimate it as halfway between a tertiary division. It is reasonable to try to estimate a fourth significant figure as 0 or 5.

Courtesy of Keuffel & Esser Co.
Fig. 9-6

Section three: Primary Division 4 -- Right index (See Figure 9-7):

Courtesy of Keuffel & Esser Co.
Fig. 9-7

As with the two previous sections of the scale, there are ten secondary divisions between each primary division. However, the space between each secondary division is divided only into halves.   Thus between each primary division there are only 10 x 2 or 20 subparts, and each tertiary division has a value of 5.   Therefore we may set the third significant figure precisely on a mark only if it is a 0 or 5; otherwise it must be estimated.   One should not attempt to set a fourth figure on this part of the scale.

Locating Numbers on the C and D Scales

Once the number divisions of the C and D scales are understood it is easy to locate numbers on them.   Some examples are given below:

SINGLE-DIGIT NUMBERS

Single-digit numbers are located on the Primary Divisions:

TWO-DIGIT NUMBERS

Two-digit numbers are located on the Secondary Divisions.

THREE-DIGIT NUMBERS

Three-digit numbers are located on or between the Tertiary Divisions.

EXAMPLE: Find the three-digit number, 246.

MORE THAN THREE DIGITS

Numbers with more than three digits need only be set to the third or fourth place, since the percentage of error in your final answer will be so tiny that it will be insignificant in most problems.

Thus, the number 186,530 should be called 186,500 and set as follows:

Courtesy of Keuffel & Esser Co.
Fig. 9-8

Learning to locate numbers on the C-D scale quickly and accurately comes with practice. The best procedure is to work multiplication and division problems to which the answer is known or given. This provides a built-in check that will enable one to correct his mistakes without the aid of a teacher. There are hundreds of such problems in the books listed at the end of this section. Certain mathematical tables will also provide plenty of practice. Or one can make up his own problems.

Placing the Decimal Point

In using a slide rule, the decimal point of the answer must be placed by estimation. This is accomplished by working the problem mentally or, if necessary, on paper with each number rounded to one significant figure. Suppose we are multiplying 1372 by 365. We say to ourselves 1000 x 400 is 400,000. Since the slide rule answer is the digits 501, we then know that the answer is 501,000. If the numbers had been 13.72 and 36.5, we would have thought: 10 x 40 is 400 and known that the answer was 501.

Multiplication

    1. Pull the indicator along the D scale until the hairline is exactly on top of (in register with) one of the numbers to be multiplied.

    2. Push the central sliding part of the rule until the left index of the C scale is also under the hairline.

    3. Pull the indicator along the C scale until the hairline is in register with the other number being multiplied. (This number on the C scale may be beyond the right index of the D scale. If so, simply reverse the C scale by putting the right C index under the hairline in place of the left one. The required number on C will then also be on the D range).

Example: 18 x 26 (See Figure 9-9).

Courtesy of Keuffel & Esser Co.
Fig. 9-9

Division

    1. Pull the hairline in register with the dividend on the D scale.

    2. Push the divisor under the hairline on the C scale.

    3. Pull the hairline to whichever C index is over the D scale.

    4. Read the quotient under the hairline on the D scale.

Example: 875 / 35 (See Figure 9-10).

Courtesy of Keuffel & Esser Co.
Fig. 9-10

Application of Slide Rule Multiplication and Division to the Problems Presented in This Book

Example 1. Convert seconds to hundredths of a minute.

The formula is: Hundredths of a minute = 5/3 x seconds.

1. Push the hairline to 5 on the D scale.

2. Pull 3 on the C scale under the hairline.

3. Push the hairline to the given number of seconds on the C scale.

Note: Since 5/3 is not the final answer, it is <u>not</u> necessary to push the hairline to the left or right index to read the quotient.

4. Read the answer under the hairline on the D scale. If necessary, reverse the indexes as explained in the section on multiplication. For values under 60 seconds reversal will not be necessary.

Note: Once the first two steps are performed, any number of conversions may be performed without repeating them. For example, if in step 3 the hairline is pushed to 22 seconds on C, the answer on D (to the nearest hundredth) is 37 hundredths of a minute. If we then want also to convert 13 seconds, we merely push the hairline to 13 on C and read 22 hundredths of a minute on D -- that is, we repeat step 3 with a different value.

Example 2. Solve the either-or sample size formula.

The formula is: $N' = \dfrac{1600 \ (1 - P)}{P}$

1. Push the hairline to 1600 on the D scale.

2. Pull the value for P on the C scale under the hairline.

3. Push the hairline to the (1 - P) value on the C scale.

4. Read the answer under the hairline on the D scale.

For example, if P = 18% (i.e., 0.18 for slide rule purposes), N' = 1600 (0.82)/0.18, or 7289 observations.

Example 3. Solve the sample size formula,

$$N' = \frac{1600 \left[N \underset{\sim}{\Sigma} X^2 - \left(\underset{\sim}{\Sigma} X \right)^2 \right]}{\left(\underset{\sim}{\Sigma} X \right)^2}$$

We must first perform the subtraction longhand (one cannot add or subtract on a slide rule). But once this is done the remaining expression -- the time-consuming one -- is easily solved on the slide rule:

1. Push the hairline to 1600 on the D scale.

2. Pull the value for $(\leqslant X)^2$ on the C scale under the hairline.

3. Push the hairline to the $N \leqslant X^2 - (\leqslant X)^2$ value on the C scale.

4. Read the answer under the hairline on the D scale.

Bibliography

Checking Arithmetic
Mueller, Francis J. Arithmetic: Its Structure and Concepts. Englewood Cliffs, N. J. : Prentice-Hall, 1956.

The Trachtenberg Speed System of Basic Mathematics. Translated and adapted by Ann Cutler and Rudolph McShane. Garden City, N. Y. , Doubleday, 1960.

Slide Rule
Ellis, John P. The Theory and Operation of the Slide Rule. New York: Dover, 1961.

Harris, Charles O. Slide Rule Simplified. 2nd ed. Chicago: American Technical Society, 1961.

Kells, Lyman M. , Kern, Willis F. , and Bland, James R. K + E Log Log Duplex Decitrig Slide Rule No. N4081; Manual. New York: Keuffel and Esser Co. , 1947.

Keuffel and Esser Company. Learning to Use the Slide Rule... Instructions for the K12 Prep Slide Rule. New York: Keuffel and Esser Co. , 1961.

Perrine, James O. The Slide Rule Handbook. Baywood Publishing Co. Distributed by Gordon and Breach, 1965.

Saffold, Robert, and Smalley, Ann. The Slide Rule. Prepared under the direction of Education Science Division, U. S. Industries, Inc. Garden City, N.Y. : Doubleday, 1962.

Chapter **X**
Cost

Unit Cost

Every administrator should be able to determine the cost of operation of his library. There is more than one way to consider cost. It is possible, for example, to consider cost distinct from production. Thus if a person works forty hours per week for the library, and his salary cost to the library is $2.00 an hour, then his labor cost per week to the library is 40 x $2.00, or $80.00. This type of information provides an administrator with data on overall organizational cost; but it does not provide any guidance concerning costs in relation to useful work produced. For example, an employee might produce at a high rate or an average rate, or he might be an inveterate loafer who devoted the bulk of his time to sitting with his feet up on his desk, twiddling his thumbs. An employee might be eager to work, but not be able to because a machine broke down, or he had to wait on someone else to complete his function first, or the like. General hourly rates cannot measure the impact of these or similar variables.

The basis of relating production to cost is the unit cost. This is the cost to an organization per unit of accomplishment. Any convenient unit may be chosen. Thus in a catalog department a reasonable unit might be a cataloged book; in the circulation department, a book circulated; in the reference department, a reference question asked and/or answered. A unit cost is obtained by dividing the total cost of producing a given number of units by the number of units produced. A unit cost is thus an average cost. The formula is:

$$\text{Unit cost} = \frac{\text{Cost of Producing N Units of Work}}{\text{N}}$$

This unit cost is the basis of cost accounting. It allows an organization to compare its performance with the performance of

150

others engaged in similar work, and to compare its performance
for one period with another period.   Unit costs also provide a certain power of prediction.   For instance, assume that a state aca-
demic institution is suddenly ordered to begin several new graduate
programs for the following year and that the state has promised to
support these new programs with additional book funds.   However,
the state has made no financial provision for processing the additional library materials that will be required.   The librarian realizes that unless he moves quickly there is a strong likelihood that
the needed processing monies will not be forthcoming; so he requests his processing administrator to gather factual cost data for
presentation to the administration of the university.

Fortunately, the processing administrator is cost conscious
and knows that his unit cost for ordering a book is $x.xx, for cat-
aloging it is $y.yy, and for labelling, binding, and shelving it is
$z.zz.   He also knows the average purchase price of a book for
the library.   He divides this figure into the amount of money by
which the state has said it will increase the book budget and finds
that the increase will allow the library to purchase about 15,000
more books next year.   Armed with these data the librarian will
be able to demonstrate that processing an additional 15,000 books
will require ($x.xx + $y.yy + $z.zz) x 15,000.

Labor Cost

Labor is generally the heaviest expense in the library budget.
For management study purposes it is important to recognize that
labor cost per productive hour is not merely the product of: paid
time on the job x employee's hourly wage.   This is due to the fact
that: 1) companies commonly make additional contributions to the
account of the employee, and 2) employees do not work all the time
for which they are paid.   For 1) an employer usually contributes
to social security and often to insurance and pension costs, and the
like.   With regard to 2) an employee expects to be paid for vaca-
tions, holidays, sick leave, and rest periods.   Thus:

Labor cost per   Salary cost + Additional cost
Productive hour = Number of hours actually devoted to productive
                                                               work

As an example, let us suppose that a professional cataloger in a public library receives a salary of $6000.00 a year. He works a 40-hour week. The cataloger is paid for all 52 weeks of the year: 40 hours x 52 weeks = 2080 hours paid for the year. If he worked this full time and cost the library no more than his salary, then he would cost the library $6000.00/2080, or $2.88 per productive hour.

But in order to produce a realistic per hour charge, several additional costs must be added to the minimum charge of $2.88. The 1965 social security (F.I.C.A.) rate was 3.625% on the first $4800.00 of annual income. Thus the library must contribute $4800.00 x 0.03625 = $174.00 or the equivalent of one and one-half week's pay.

Beyond social security, employer's contributions are less standardized but may include such items as retirement plans, insurance policies of various sorts, bonuses, and so on, and labor contracts are placing more and more emphasis upon such "fringe benefits." For our purposes, let us say that the library's contribution totals about 4% of the cataloger's salary; $6000.00 x 0.04 = $240.00. The total additional cost is then $174.00 + $240.00 or $414.00.

In order to determine the productive labor cost it is still necessary to ascertain the number of hours actually worked in a year. To do this it will be necessary to determine the number of hours not worked and subtract this value from the number of hours paid for, which as already known is 2080 hours. Practically all librarians receive at least two weeks paid vacation per year, and many receive a month or more. For illustration, let us assume that our cataloger receives three weeks paid vacation per year, which amounts to 40 x 3 = 120 hours. The library also bears the expense for paid holidays and our cataloger is granted nine holidays. These nine paid holidays amount to seventy-two hours (9 x 8 hours). Some librarians have not missed a day of work, or taken a single day of sick leave, in 35 years. However, the overwhelming majority of workers have. Our average cataloger will miss some work time due to illness. We shall estimate this conservatively at one week, or 40 hours, per year.

As discussed in the time study chapter (Chapter VII), most library employees are granted fatigue allowances and an allowance for personal needs. Two twenty minute coffee breaks per day (2/3 of an hour) and twenty minutes for personal needs per day (1/3 of an hour) were cited as typical for libraries. With no time off our cataloger would work 260 days per year (52 x 5 = 260 days); but from this must be subtracted 15 days for vacation, and 9 days for holidays, and 5 days for sick leave: 260 - (15 + 5 + 9) = 231 days worked per year. The total hours to be subtracted as non-productive paid time are thus:

Vacation	120 hours	(15 x 8 hours)
Holidays	72 hours	(9 x 8 hours)
Sickness	40 hours	(5 x 8 hours)
Rest	154 hours	(231 x 2/3 hours)
Personal	77 hours	(231 x 1/3 hours)
	463 hours	

The number of hours that our cataloger actually works is 2080 - 463, or 1617 hours per year. We are now able to substitute into the formula:

$$\frac{\text{Labor cost per}}{\text{Productive hour}} = \frac{\text{Salary cost + Additional cost}}{\text{No. of hours actually devoted to productive work}}$$

$$\frac{\text{Labor cost per}}{\text{Productive hour}} = \frac{\$6000.00 + \$414.00}{1617} = \$3.97 \text{ per productive hr.}$$

This cost represents a significant increase of $1.09 or 38 per cent over the original unadjusted figure of $2.88. For really accurate unit costs we should also add space costs, equipment depreciation and maintenance, supplies, supervisory costs, time spent on conferences with supervisors or in staff meetings, etc. so the actual cost per hour of time will frequently be close to twice the hourly salary.

Depreciation Cost

The library profession has been slow generally to recognize the importance of depreciation. For our purposes depreciation may be defined as allowances made for decreases in value of equipment due to obsolescence, wear, or deterioration. This failure to use

depreciation costs can be attributed to two causes: first, libraries
until recently did not have to invest heavily for equipment; and second, and probably more important, libraries for the most part are
tax-supported, non-profit institutions which have not kept cost records.

Libraries are not as fully mechanized as most industries;
nonetheless, they do require a considerable variety and quantity of
equipment. For example, desks and tables, chairs, typewriters,
charging machines, shelving, card catalog cabinets, book trucks,
elevators and conveyors, file cabinets, map cases, film and film-
strip projectors, microfilm, microprint and microcard readers, reproducing equipment (such as Thermofax, Verifax, Xerox), and the
microforms, films, records, and books themselves are all required. For the purposes of this section, the library building itself, if it is not being rented, may also be regarded as a piece of
equipment. The trend today is for a library to allocate an increasingly larger portion of its annual budget to equipment expenditures. This trend is being spurred in some cases by automation
and the adoption of data processing equipment for library operations.

Business and industry must regard depreciation from two
points of view. First, the rate of depreciation has a significant effect on the amount of tax paid the government and thus on corpor-
ate profits. Generally speaking, the higher the depreciation rate
allowed, the lower the taxes. Second, regardless of taxes, depreciation is an important tool of management. Even if a businessman
were able to convince the Internal Revenue Service that a certain
rate of depreciation was valid, or at least technically allowable, he
would still need to know the true (as distinct from "book") rate in
order to plan his business intelligently, for it is on the basis of the
true rate of depreciation that he must plan to have funds available
for replacement of worn out equipment. Libraries, being non-profit institutions, do not have to worry about taxes; but they, like industry, are concerned with equipment purchases and replacement.

In addition to management study applications, depreciation
data, if skillfully employed, can prove to be a powerful ally to a

library administrator struggling to justify expenditures for equipment. It has been common for libraries to consider equipment purchases as current expenditures. Unfortunately this practice creates a fallacious picture. When the purchase is carried as a current expenditure, there is an implication that its usefulness will end with the current fiscal period. This ignores the reality that a piece of equipment may have a useful life of many years. For example, if some libraries were to request the purchase of two typewriters which cost a total of $800.00, the necessary cash outlay might seem prohibitive to a budgeting official. However, the machines will have a useful life expectancy of ten or more years; therefore, the typewriters will cost actually only one-tenth, or less, of their purchase price each year. Another way of approaching this question is to point out that if the library were to close its doors, the typewriters would still possess a salvage value depending on their age and condition.

There are several depreciation models from which to choose. For management purposes the best model is the one which is not overly cumbersome but which still provides a reasonably close representation of the facts. In this chapter two of the most common models are described. Each model has its own desirable and undesirable features, and each presents depreciation data differently.

"Straight-Line" Depreciation

The simplest model is known as "straight-line" depreciation. The name arises from the fact that when dollars are plotted against years on Cartesian coordinates, the resultant graph is a straight line (See Figure 10-1). The formula for this model is:

$$\text{Amount of depreciation per year} = \frac{\text{Purchase Price} - \text{Salvage value of item at time of replacement}}{\text{Number of years between purchase and replacement}}$$

The use of this model can be illustrated by the following example. Four years ago a library purchased a table-model reproducing machine of well-known name for $509.65. The machine still operates satisfactorily. However, due to rapid technological advance in the field, the newest model of this machine is much improved, and the library is therefore interested in trading in the old machine toward the purchase of a new model. The company will allow a trade-in value of $100.00 for the old machine. In this case the depreciation formula will be:

$$\text{Depreciation} = \frac{\$509.65 - \$100.00}{4} = \$102.41 \text{ per year}$$

Once the amount of depreciation to allow per year is known, it is then possible to prepare a depreciation schedule. For our example, this schedule would be:

Year	Book value at beginning of year	Annual Depreciation	Book value at end of year
1st	$509.65	$ 102.41	$407.24
2nd	407.24	102.41	304.83
3rd	304.83	102.41	202.42
4th	202.42	102.41	100.01

Sum of Years Depreciation

Some persons object to using the straight-line depreciation model on the grounds that it is not sufficiently consonant with reality for the first few years. Straight-line allows the same amount of depreciation for the first as the last year. However, the rate of depreciation usually tends to be higher for the first few years. Various depreciation models have been developed in an attempt to overcome this limitation. One of the most common is the sum of years model. To make comparison easy, the data used with the straight-line method will be repeated. The depreciation schedule for the sum of years model is shown below:

Year	Reversed Year	Reversed Year/Sum	Book value at Beginning of Yr.	Annual Depreciation	Book value at end of year
1	4	4/10	$509.65	$163.86	$345.79
2	3	3/10	345.79	122.90	222.89
3	2	2/10	222.89	81.93	140.96
4	1	1/10	140.96	40.96	100.00
Sum = 10				$409.65	

The step-by-step procedure for constructing the depreciation table is:

1. Estimate the number of years between purchase and need for replacement -- in the example, four -- and write the figures from one to this number in a column in ascending order ("Year" column of schedule).

2. Write these same numbers in reverse or descending order in the next column and add them. In the example, the sum is ten. For a larger number of years, the sum could be found by use of the formula N $(N + 1)/2$, where N is the number of years. Thus: $4(4 + 1)2 = 10$. ("Reversed year" column).

3. For each year divide the "Reversed year" value by the sum of the years. (See "Reversed Year/Sum" column.) Note that for each succeeding year the fraction has a smaller value.

4. Subtract the Salvage value from the Purchase price. In the example this value is $409.65 ($509.65 - $100.00 = $409.65). For each year multiply the difference by the "Reversed Year/Sum" fraction for that year. This will yield the amount of depreciation to be allowed for that year (See "Annual depreciation" column). In the example, the depreciation for the first year would be $409.65 x 4/10 or $163.86; for the second year, $409.65 x 3/10 or $122.90; and so on. The general formula is: Depreciation for year = (Purchase price - Salvage value) x ("Reversed" value for year/Sum of years). The correctness of the arithmetic may be checked by adding all the values in the depreciation column. The sum should (within rounding errors) equal: Purchase price - Salvage value.

5. The book value columns are completed by means of subtraction. Thus in the example for the first year: $509.65 - $163.86 = $345.79; for the second year, $345.79 - $122.90 = $222.89; and so on. The final subtraction should (within rounding errors) yield a remainder equal to the salvage value.

The straight-line and sum of years models are compared graphically in Figure 10-1. The different depreciation rates are clearly visible from the chart. The straight-line model is easier to use, and will be acceptable for most library studies. By comparison, the sum of years model usually presents a more realistic picture, but is a little more difficult to calculate. The choice between these two methods will depend on the circumstances and purposes of a particular study.

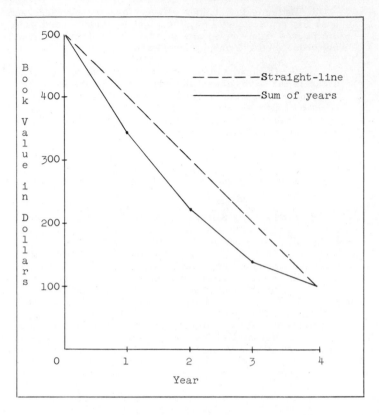

Fig. 10-1 Comparison of straight-line and sum of year
depreciation schedules for office photo-copier.

Original Cost Versus Replacement Cost

The price of equipment has been increasing for many years.
The cost of replacing an item when it is worn out or obsolete will
probably be higher than the original cost. If an item is depreciated over a long period -- a library building might be depreciated
over about fifty years -- then the discrepancy between the two costs
will be substantial. To compensate for this difference and have
enough money available for replacement when it is needed business
firms sometimes charge a higher depreciation rate against current
income than would be justified in terms of original cost. For
non-profit, tax-supported organizations funds are usually not set

aside in this manner. Current expense, including routine, minor
equipment addition and replacement, is covered by the current
budget. As current expenses increase from year to year, so do
taxes. Major capital improvements (such as new library buildings)
are usually financed, as needed, by long term bond issues. But
even though it is somewhat disguised by city, county, state and fed-
eral fiscal techniques, the librarian should be aware that higher replacement cost is an unpleasant reality.

Estimating Useful Life of Equipment

Of course if it is to be used for planning purposes, depreciation must be estimated before, instead of after, the fact. Here
the guideline must be the previously recorded experience of seemingly comparable situations. If the appropriate data cannot be determined from one's own records, a library may still turn to the
experience of others. In 1942 the Internal Revenue Service published its Bulletin F: Income tax depreciation and obsolescence
estimated useful lives and depreciation rates, which remained the
standard depreciation guide for the next two decades. It included
detailed tables of the average useful lives (in years) of virtually
every important type of equipment, including buildings. In 1962
the Internal Revenue Service, for a variety of reasons, including a
desire to encourage the sale of capital equipment and stimulate the
economy, collected the hundreds of individual items of equipment
into a relatively few type-of-business groupings. In general the new
rules provide just one average useful life figure (decreasing the life
for some items and increasing it for others) for a group of similar
items that had previously been listed individually. In addition, the
average useful life has been shortened from about 19 years (in
Bulletin F) to 13 years. (For the new rules, see: Depreciation
guidelines and rules, IRS publ. 456. Second Printing. Sept., 1962.)

In order to understand the changes clearly, a librarian may
wish to compare the "Office equipment" section of Bulletin F with
the "Office furniture, fixtures, machines and equipment" section of
the new rules, where he will observe that the allowable composite
life of library-type equipment has been reduced from 15 to 10 years.

There is no question that even from the point of view of a tax exempt institution the new procedure has its advantages -- for example, vastly simplified depreciation bookkeeping. At the same time, however, changing the average useful life in print does not change it in fact, and for certain management purposes, a librarian may still prefer to use Bulletin F, or better still, his own library's recorded experience.

Cost of Maintenance of Equipment

Maintenance of equipment is sometimes a significant additional expense. If a piece of equipment is complex and essential to library operation, it usually pays the library to procure an annual service contract with the manufacturer or some other firm to guarantee that the equipment will be kept operational by systematic preventative maintenance and, when necessary, prompt repair. A typical library example is given in the Equipment Costs Table (Figure 13-7) of Chapter XIII. A Remington Rand Champion Microfilmer costing $1310.00 is amortized over 10 years by the straight-line method -- that is, at $131.00 per year (assuming no salvage value). However, to this figure must be added an annual service charge of $110.00 making a total annual cost of $131.00 + $110.00 or $241.00. Sometimes libraries choose to rent rather than buy equipment. Service is usually included in the rental cost.

Supply Cost

For most libraries the calculation of supply costs is a reasonably simple undertaking. Drawing either from the experience of one's own institution or from that of others, it is possible to estimate the number of units of a particular supply that will be used in a given period. The cost of the supply item for the given period then is:

Cost of supply = Unit cost x Number of units

To take a case, suppose we wished to order 24,000 catalog cards and decided that a given supplier's medium weight, 50% rag content cards are of sufficiently high quality for our needs. Checking this suppliers catalog, we find that these cards are $4.95 per 1000 if more than 10,000 cards are purchased at one time. Therefore, using 1000 cards as our unit:

Cost of cards = $4.95 x 24 = $118.80

Purchasing supplies in quantity will often produce a worthwhile discount for the library. In the above example, if the library
had purchased less than 10,000 cards, the cost would have been
$5.25 per 1000 rather than $4.95 per 1000. Ordering in smaller
lots also costs in other ways. Each order must be handled separately by the library (both in sending and receiving) as well as by
the supplier. This requires time, and labor time sooner or later
must be translated into dollars.

With quantity purchasing there is always the question: How
much should be purchased? What is the optimum amount? This
is not an easy question to answer. In fact, it is in an effort to
answer just such questions that industry has developed special operation research techniques. For library purposes, the most practical approach is to estimate the number of units that will be used
in the forseeable future, assuming that cost is not prohibitive and
storage space is readily available. It is generally unwise to invest
in large purchases when a library procedure is in a state of flux.
For example, it would be foolish to purchase a year's supply of
edged-notched cards for a circulation system while an evaluation
that might alter the system was in progress.

Finally, some mention should be made of storage costs. As
will be seen from the ensuing section, space costs money. Buildings must either be rented or purchased and, in either case, maintained -- heated, lighted, cleaned, and so on. Therefore, to store
large quantities of supplies (or equipment) long before they are
needed is an expense. Money spent in anticipation could have been
invested in other ways, perhaps earning interest, for the interim.
One of the reasons why libraries which are too large are rarely
built is because the funds needed for the unused space can be more
profitably invested in other ways.

General Cost

General costs are those which are not ordinarily charged directly as belonging exclusively to the particular part of the library

operation being costed. Salary, depreciation, and supply costs
must, in certain cases, be considered as general costs. For instance, administrators usually divide their time among several different library activities. If one is costing an activity that directly
involves the time of an administrator, then his salary should be included as one of the general costs. Other general library costs
which have not yet been discussed are rent, cleaning, lighting,
heating, air conditioning, telephone, repairs, and insurance.

General expenses vary relatively little with the amount of
business done. It should, for example, cost about the same to
light a library with only a few patrons using it as to light the same
library filled to capacity. In contrast, specific, direct costs tend
to vary in relatively direct proportion to the volume of work done.
An example would be the salaries of catalogers. The more books
to be cataloged, the more catalogers are required. In this sense
general expenses are sometimes referred to as fixed costs, and
specific expenses as variable costs.

For management study purposes the important point to remember is that in costing a particular library function, general
costs should not be ignored. Rather, a just proportion of them
should be charged to the particular function. The general formula
is:

General cost to be charged to   Total general cost x Percentage
the function being studied   =   of general cost properly
                                     chargeable to the function
                                     being studied

As an example, suppose that the head of an Acquisitions Department
whose salary is $10,000 per year devotes on the average 20% of
his time to the Order Section. Then 0.20 x $10,000 or $2000 of
his salary should be charged against the Order Section.

Each of the other general expenses should be allocated on
whatever seems to be the most reasonable basis. The heating bill
might be prorated on the basis of cubic feet; the lighting bill on
the basis of square feet; the telephone bill on the basis of the number of instruments. Custodial service, fire and theft insurance,
and building depreciation or rental would normally be allocated on
the basis of square feet. If a scale floor plan is available (the

architect's drawings, or the like), it is easy to compute area from it.   Figure 10-2 is an example of a scale diagram of a single room divided for an actual management study into several rather small sub-areas on the basis of function.   The numbers represent square feet.

It is sometimes interesting and useful to study the general costs of others.   One of the most reputable and enduring of such records in print is that of the Annual Experience Exchange Report, prepared by the Philadelphia Building Owners and Managers Associ-

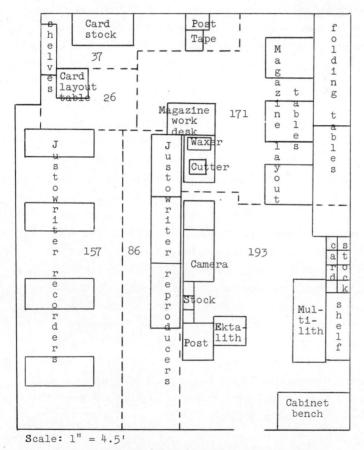

Scale: 1" = 4.5'

Fig. 10-2 A composing room divided for management
purposes into sub-areas on the basis of function.

ation. This report is printed in each November issue of: Buildings, the Construction and Building Managment Journal (Stamats
Publishing Co.).   For a portion of the 1963 report (printed in November, 1964) see Figure 10-3.   It includes the total operating expenses for thirty-four Philadelphia office buildings.   The average
1963 cost per square foot of rental area was $3. 479.   This total
cost is broken down in considerable detail.   The greatest single
cost is building depreciation ($0. 849 per rentable square foot in
1963).   Of course, rental rates vary from section to section of the
country and from year to year, and most libraries are not office-
type buildings.   Taxes are not a factor with libraries either.   Nontheless, the librarian should find it of interest to examine the rela-
tive magnitude of the different costs.

Total Cost

For clarity and convenience, labor, depreciation, supply,
and general costs have been discussed separately.   Now it is both
appropriate and important to emphasize the importance of adding
them together to achieve a total systems cost.   If a cost is omitted
the analyst must be certain that its omission will not have a significant effect on the result.   To omit costs carelessly is to delude
oneself that the cost of an operation is less than it really is.   Depreciation and other general costs in particular tend to be ignored
or overlooked.   However, even though they can be difficult to compute, general costs are as real as labor and supply costs and are
often of significant magnitude.   It is an easy thing to use inadequate or unintentionally biased cost figures to reinforce a natural
desire for low costs if such costs will put an operation in a favor-
able light.   The principle to remember is that one cannot include
a cost which has been overlooked.   This is why it is necessary to
analyze the operation thoroughly before costing it.   A library example incorporating labor, equipment, supply, and general costs is
presented in Chapter XIII.

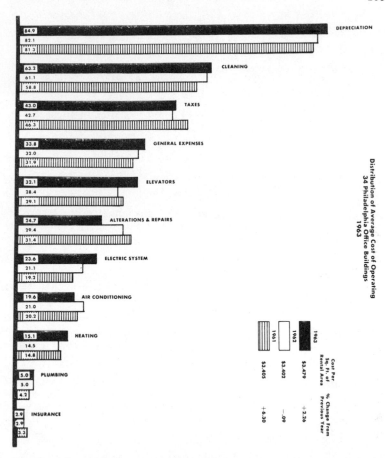

Fig. 10-3 Operating Costs of 34 Philadelphia Office Buildings in
1963.   Philadelphia Building Owners and Managers Association, "Annual Experience Exchange Report," Buildings,
LVIII, No. 11, (November, 1964), p. 72. Courtesy Buildings Magazine.

Bibliography

Cost Accounting
Dickey, Robert I., ed.   Accountants' Cost Handbook.   2nd ed.
New York: Ronald, 1960.

Schiff, Michael, and Benninger, Lawrence J.   Cost Accounting.
2nd ed.   New York: Ronald, 1963.

Depreciation

Committee on Mathematics of Finance. Mathematics of Finance.
New York: Pitman, 1958. Chapter 9, "Depreciation."

Internal Revenue Service. Depreciation Guidelines and Rules.
Washington, D. C. : U. S. Government Printing Office, 1962.
(IRS Publication 456).

Internal Revenue Service. Income Tax Depreciation and Obsoles-
ence Estimated Useful Lives and Depreciation Rates. Washington, D. C. : U. S. Government Printing Office, 1942.
(IRS Bulletin F).

Grant, Eugene L. , and Norton Jr. , Paul T. Depreciation. Rev.
Printing. New York: Ronald, 1955.

Mouzon, Edwin D. , and Rees, Paul K. Mathematics of Finance.
Boston: Allyn and Bacon, 1959. Chapter 14, "Depreciation
and Capitalized Cost."

General Costs

Brummet, R. Lee. Overhead Costing: the Costing of Manufactured Products. Ann Arbor: Bureau of Business Research,
School of Business Administration, University of Michigan,
1957. (Michigan Business Studies, XIII, No. 2).

Heyel, Carl, ed. The Encyclopedia of Management. New York:
Reinhold, 1963. Article on "Overhead Assignment," p. 636-
42.

Philadelphia Building Owners and Managers Association. Annual
Experience Exchange Report. Appears in each November
issue of Buildings, the Construction and Building Management Journal. Stamats Publishing Co.

Libraries

Baldwin, Emma V. , and Marcus, William E. Library Costs and
Budgets: a Study of Cost Accounting in Public Libraries.
New York: Bowker, 1941.

Brutcher, Constance, Gessford, Glen, and Rixford, Emmet.
"Cost Accounting for the Library," Library Resources and
Technical Services, VIII, No. 4 (Fall, 1964), p. 413-31.

Heinritz, Fred J. Book Versus Card Catalog Costs. Ph. D. Dissertation. Rutgers, the State University, 1963. Available
from University Microfilms.

Wight, Edmund A. Public Library Finance and Accounting.
Chicago: American Library Association, 1943. Chapter 7,
"Cost Accounting."

The catalogs of the following organizations contain a considerable amount of useful management information on library-type supply and equipment specifications and cost:

Bro-Dart Industries

Demco Library Supplies

Gaylord Brothers

Goldsmith Brothers

Library Bureau (of Remington Rand)

For articles consult Library Literature under the heading:

Time and Cost Studies.

Chapter XI
Performance Standards and Control

A performance standard (sometimes called a work standard) is a means of measuring the quantity of work produced by a person working at a normal pace under normal conditions. This seems straightforward; but nontheless performance standards and other measures for control are a source of general misunderstanding. Although they have been discussed in library literature, they have not yet gained wide on-the-job acceptance in libraries. In addition to quantitative controls, quality measures or quality control must be given careful consideration. This tool is an almost untapped library management resource. There are numerous library procedures amenable to qualitative measurement. Finally, recognition must also be given to standardization of methods and equipment. Standardization has been the foundation for the before-mentioned controls. It has made possible much of the technological progress of the twentieth century. Without it, mass production would not be possible.

Standardization

The objective of standardization is to eliminate useless, wasteful and disadvantageous diversity. Occasionally misunderstanding will arise between the terms "standardization" and "performance standards." Standardization is usually used in the context of uniformity, whereas performance standards refer to output goals such as the number of catalog cards filed per hour.

By eliminating wasteful variation, standardization facilitates interchangeability. This can be illustrated by the design of a typewriter keyboard; imagine the chaos that would ensue if each manufacturer pursued his own keyboard style. Or imagine the impact if libraries used different sized catalog cards instead of accepting one standard size. Inspection would be impossible without some basic standardization. Standardization of library equipment, materials, and methods has gained rather wide acceptance in theory but rather limited implementation in practice. However, there are a few examples that can be pointed out: the catalog card, some furniture dimensions, the ALA interlibrary loan form. Standardization of methods also facilitates training of new employees. Without procedural standardization it would not be practical to prepare procedure manuals because a job might be performed differently each cycle, day, or week.

Standardization in Libraries

Standardization of human activities, operations, tools, forms, records and materials is a fundamental prerequisite to scientific management. Librarians have long been congnizant of its importance; but advances have been painfully slow. Statistics are often cited to compare costs, collections, personnel, etc. However, the data are usually not comparable because the raw data reported by the participating institutions are not comparable; such statistics can provide the profession only with gross approximations. Unless operations are performed identically and statistical bases for reporting data are uniform, there is little valid basis for comparison. The pattern of library development throughout the country has produced more examples of rugged individualism than of uniformity. Since the die has already been cast, the obstacles to standardization will be even more formidable than if the profession were now beginning fresh.

Approaches to Standardization

Standardization can be approached either on a local or regional basis or on a national scale. Many libraries are concentrating on increasing uniformity within a single system, be it a city, county, region, or state. Uniform order forms, borrowers' cards, interlibrary loan forms are replacing diverse local products. Regional processing centers have also brought some measure of standardization.

Efforts to standardize on a national scale include such programs as quality of library bindings, durability of book paper, and

development of a single system for transliterating Cyrillic letters
into the Roman alphabet. Some of these programs have emanated
from within the American Library Association, while others have
been stimulated through cooperative efforts under the American
Standards Association, Committee Z-39.

New technological advances dictate a new urgency for standardization. For example, computer programs have evolved almost
at random to the extent that many programs are not compatible
with the equipment of competitors. Initially this might have been
advantageous, but it has now become a burden to manufacturers as
well as users. Although some efforts to improve the situation have
been made, the picture is still far from bright.

Performance Standards

Performance standards are an aid to management in both
planning and controlling activities. They can furnish data on man-
power requirements, and on the number of employees required to
perform a prescribed volume of work. They can improve planning
and scheduling of work. They can be used to determine the requirements to perform a prescribed volume of work. Work loads
can be balanced so that the work of one department does not become out of phase with related units. Standards can be employed
in measuring and controlling costs. Finally, standards can provide
added rationality to a personnel program. Workers can be told
what is expected of them, and personnel officers can gain a clearer
understanding of the duties and requirements of a job.

Suitability of Standards to Library Work

Although few libraries have adopted performance standards,
they are applicable to library jobs. Standards may be developed
for any task quantitatively measurable. Included are all mechanical, routine, and repetitive jobs, many examples of which may be
found in circulation, book ordering, and processing. It has been
estimated that from 60 to 90 per cent of all library work is quanti-
fiable routine work. In spite of the failure of the profession to tap
this potential source of objective standardization data, subjective
standards are constantly used by supervisors. If a supervisor be-

comes dissatisfied with an employee's performance, the implication
is that the worker has failed to meet some prescribed level. When
the employee is confronted with this criticism, he may logically
seek to learn what level of production would be satisfactory. A supervisor may be hard pressed for a rational response.

As work calls increasingly for judgment and professional
knowledge, quantitative measurement becomes more difficult and
less precise.   It has been said that all human activity could be
measured, if we possessed sufficiently precise measuring tools.
However, until theoretical capabilities such as these can be trans-
formed into reality, certain aspects of such professional activities
as reference service, reader's services, and bibliographic work will
continue to defy precise measurement.

Methods of Setting Standards

Standards can be established in several different ways.
They may be based on production statistics of past performance,
work sampling data, time study data, standard time data, or subjective measures, (if these latter can be truly labelled standards).
The degree of precision achieved by these different methods obviously varies; it does not necessarily follow, however, that the pre-
ferred method will always by synonymous with accuracy or precision.   Common sense and the needs of the job will play major
roles in deciding the appropriate method.

Before any standard can be set, measurable work units must
be identified, defined, and standardized.   Some commonly used library work units include title, volume, catalog cards, books circulated, and reference questions asked.   An unambiguously defined
work unit is the basis for work measurement, evaluation, and comparison.

Let us now examine in turn the various methods of setting
standards:

1) Production records.   Standards based on production statistics are compiled from employee production records, or from
production records of an administrative unit.   These standards are
based on what has been accomplished and not on what can be ac-

complished, which limits their usefulness. This approach is not at all scientific nor are the results. On the other hand, it does not require a great deal of judgment to establish production standards, and for many situations they can be introduced as a starting point upon which all concerned can agree.

2) Work sampling. Work sampling is discussed in Chapter VIII. In addition to the uses already cited work sampling data can be converted into standards. For example, suppose we wished to study the time required to file cards in a catalog. We would learn from work sampling observations the per cent of time spent actually filing during the work time allotted to filing. Then, since we know the time devoted to filing, the amount of time for worker allowances, and the number of cards filed, we can calculate an average time for filing cards into the catalog. Suppose that the filer was observed to be actually filing during 75% of the times observed, that the time devoted to filing was 480 minutes, that the personal allowance was 30 minutes, and that 500 cards were filed. Then:

$0.75 \times (480-30)$ Minutes $= 322$ minutes actually filing.

322 minutes $\times 1/500$ cards filed $= 0.65$ minutes per card filed.

Standards constructed from work sampling data embody the same limitation as standards based on production records. The measurement is based not on what can be performed but rather on what has been performed.

3) Time study data. The most reliable standards are those based on time study data. Time study work standards are also the most difficult to construct, which accounts for some of the reluctance among librarians to adopt them. The procedure for conducting a time study and converting the results into standards is discussed in Chapter VII.

4) Standard time data. Standard time data, or pre-determined time data, or motion-time-measurements (MTM) are data collected and compiled into a catalog of standard motions or tasks with times assigned to each operation. Once compiled an administrator needs only to consult the catalog to learn how much time it

will take to perform a given task. Pre-determined times have in
the past twenty years gained general acceptance in many industries.
Numerous firms are actively compiling standard times for performing different types of work. Progress has been made possible
mainly because of improved standardization.

Scant attention has been paid to the potential of standard
times for library operations until very recently. Henry Voos has
just completed a study on the premise that:

> ....those incremental items which are identical in li-
> braries can be timed. If the timing is of minute tasks
> the increments which can compose each particular li-
> brary's operation can be added to give the administrator
> some idea of how much time is spent on certain portions
> of the tasks. [1]

The catalog of times which Voos has compiled includes pasting book
pockets manually and by machine, pasting pre-gummed date due
slips, pasting pre-gummed book plates, removing dust jackets,
etc. , and he clearly demonstrates the practicality of developing
standard times especially for library tasks.

Of great importance is the standardization of library operations which already exists today. Voos concludes that:

> The time required to perform clerical routines used in
> technical processing can be predicted under many condi-
> tions and for a wide variety of machines and devices.
> It is also obvious that many of these routines are com-
> mon to a majority of libraries, whether they are public,
> college and university, school or special libraries, and
> regardless of the number of personnel on the staffs of
> these institutions. This type of micro-motion time study
> is therefore an indispensable tool for the standardization
> of statistical reporting, performance measurement, cost
> comparison, and standardization of processes. [2]

5) Subjective standards. The usual way of establishing
standards is to rely on one of a variety of subjective measures.
These subjective standards may be based on the production of the
fastest worker, group action, or personal interviews with workers.

Standards based on the production of the fastest worker necessitate observing the number of work units this individual can produce during a given period of time. This rate can then be translated into a general standard at a more reasonable rate. The pur-

pose of this approach is to demonstrate to other workers how much
work can be produced, at least by one worker, under existing conditions.   Occasionally one person out-produces his colleagues not
because he is exerting more effort than his fellow workers but because consciously or unconsciously he has developed a more efficient work method.   Once others realize why their levels are fall-
ing below his level, they may be receptive to new or different techniques.   Quantity must not, however, be confused with quality.
There are some jobs where quality is extremely important.   For
example, if a bibliographic searcher completes twice as much work
as another searcher but makes three times as many errors which
result in undesirable duplication, then a standard based solely on
production of the fastest worker would turn out to be unsatisfactory.
The nature of the job will usually dictate the type of balance needed
between quality and quantity.

Consensus standards are exemplified by our present published professional standards.   These standards are not based on
time data of any kind but rather on the pooled judgments of a group
of qualified professional librarians.   The standards are not based
on objective data because so little exists.   As a consequence, such
"standards" are a compendium of goals rather than a set of standards.   Standards resulting from group consensus can be useful.
Frequently a group through inter-change of ideas can establish the
parameters of a project.   Although the group can not produce a finished product it may provide a foundation for beginning.

Often a supervisor and an employee will work out a mutual-
ly satisfactory arrangement in a personal interview.   This may not
be in the form of explicitly stated levels.   Sometimes it will be only an understanding that so much work must be completed: for instance, all orders and letters mailed by a certain time each day,
all catalog cards filed in a given time or so many reports prepared each month.   Unless such arrangements are clearly defined
and understood, misunderstandings can arise later.   In these cases,
individuals are often hard pressed to know when they are performing
a satisfactory job.   It is not a comforting thought to be constantly
in doubt about whether the boss is pleased or dissatisfied with one's

work.

Some Rules to be Observed

A performance standard should be attainable by any worker producing at a normal pace. Moreover, it should be attainable under actual working conditions, that is, it must be translatable from the laboratory to the job.

The fact that even the most sophisticated of standards include an element of subjectivity is reason to emphasize that work standards should not become inflexible. Standards must be worked out with the full knowledge and consent (assuming a certain degree of reasonableness will be exhibited by all parties) of all those who will be laboring under their jurisdiction.

Since the purpose of standards is to provide both administrators and workers with a reasonable norm, each individual should be afforded an opportunity to demonstrate to himself that the rates are not excessive and that he can meet them without an unreasonable effort.

Once established, work standards should be permanent; they should not be changed unless or until operating conditions actually change. Change in standards should reflect either a reduction in effort or a change in the quality of supervision or of tools or of accessibility of work, etc., rather than additional expenditure of human effort. A chief cause for worker mistrust of management has stemmed from management's abuse of standards which led to the worker "slow-down," discussed in Chapter I. Standards established hastily may be either too tight or too loose. Standards which are too tight will place unreasonable demands on workers and will quickly foment dissatisfaction. Standards which are too loose will result in under-production. Inasmuch as both extremes are undesirable, rates should not be established until a thorough knowledge of the job has been gained, and whenever possible this knowledge should have been acquired through study and observation.

Standards must be comparable to be compared; they must be identical in their complexity, judgment requirements, quality requirements, and initial job qualifications. If equality does not ex-

ist, two or more standards should be established. Typing is a
task performed in all libraries. However, can we logically install
one standard for all library typing? Hardly! Typing a unit card
for the average non-fiction title is more complex than either typing a unit card for a work of fiction or typing added entries onto
a unit card. Furthermore, typing unit cards in foreign languages,
particularly in non-Roman alphabets, is more demanding than typing cards in English. For such situations libraries would have to
install at least two working standards and possibly more.

Work Standards and Professionalism

As already pointed out, some professional work is not as
yet amenable to careful measurement. However, the potentiality of
applying standards to some professional tasks should not be overlooked. As an example, cataloging and classification contain elements of both professional and nonprofessional work. Cataloging
with the aid of Library of Congress cataloging copy is normally
considered sub-professional work. Original work is viewed as professional, especially classification and assignment of subject headings. Both LC card work and original work vary in difficulty from
title to title, which renders daily or even weekly standards unreal-
istic; nevertheless, it is possible to establish meaningful standards
for cataloging over a longer period of time such as a month or
year.

Some professional librarians have objected and will probably
continue to object vociferously to work standards. They believe,
for various reasons, that standards are inappropriate for libraries.
But it should be remembered that standards do provide administrators with a rationale for planning which is of paramount importance
in this age of rapid expansion and change, and they protect staff
from unreasonable demands by supervisors.

Quality Control

Quality control in office work refers primarily to accuracy
or permissible level and scope of errors. It may also refer to effectiveness or to the manner in which work is executed. In the
latter case the concern is not whether or not the work is right or

wrong but whether it was carried out tactfully, or courteously, or in whatever manner a job might demand. Of course, the factor of effectiveness is difficult to measure because human characteristics can only be graded subjectively on an infinite continuum.

Quality control in libraries has not been implemented nearly enough. Librarians are certainly error conscious. At one time or another most librarians have spent some time revising work. Libraries usually attempt to construct a perfect card catalog, but how many libraries have been fortunate enough to achieve this goal? If there is agreement that errors are bound to occur, it would seem legitimate to query how many errors must be accepted. One might also ask whether all errors carry the same weight; for example, should an error which will probably prevent a patron from locating or identifying a desired title be treated the same as an error that will not hinder retrieval of a title? These are questions that deserve renewed thought and consideration.

Levels of Acceptable Quality.

A fundamental question that all manufacturing concerns must resolve is the dilemma of quality levels. All successful firms accept the reality that errors are bound to creep through in spite of precautions, and that some substandard products are going to reach consumers. Whenever this occurs the result is consumer dissatisfaction. Dissatisfied customers are harmful beyond their numbers.

Product guarantees are intended to minimize customer displeasure, but these measures are not completely satisfactory. On the other hand, can a company prevent all faulty products from leaving the factory without pricing themselves out of the market? One method to minimize errors is to initiate on-line inspection programs. These programs give rise to new questions. How rigorous should the inspections be, or how many times should a product be inspected? The answer to "how rigorous and how often" is not easily resolved. Since perfection is not practical, a compromise must be sought, a level that accepts some errors but not an excess.

Acceptable Level of Errors

The dilemma is in how to determine exactly what constitutes an acceptable level of error. There is no way to calculate what this level ought to be. In most cases the answer will be based on training and experience, with modifications installed later as informational feedback is obtained.

A typical library example would be reading shelves. Even if one were able to read each shelf once an hour, it would be nearly impossible to keep all the books in order all of the time. Obviously this is an extreme example. No library would attempt such an intensive program because of its prohibitive cost. Taking this illustration to the other extreme, if a shelf were read only once a year, reader dissatisfaction might become so vocal as to impair public relations. Somewhere between these two extremes the library must strive to achieve a pragmatic balance at which some books will be out of order but not enough to create general dissatisfaction.

The Nature of Errors

Errors can be categorized by type. They can be classified as substantive or nonsubstantive errors. A substantive error is one that precludes success i.e., prevents a reader from locating a book, prevents H.W. Wilson Co. from supplying the correct set of cards, etc. A nonsubstantive error is one that will detract from aesthetics of a product (card, form, books, etc.) but will not prevent success e.g., a misspelled publishers name, as McGras-Hill instead of McGraw-Hill.

How often is a revisor given instructions to distinguish between these two types of error? To take a typical case, library book orders are usually prepared by typing for distribution to vendors. In some libraries the orders are proofed before the multiform copies are separated. Assuming that it is necessary to inspect the orders at all (and this is a moot question), how will the proofing proceed? Will the revision be an attempt to produce an error-free order card, or will the revision be limited to errors that might prevent the book from being delivered or from being

paid for from the correct fund. Even if a card contained typo-
graphical errors in either or both the author and title, so long as
the errors did not impair the acquisition of the book or library
record keeping, such errors would be categorized as nonsubstantive. The crux is that errors are not all alike; and, therefore,
should not be treated alike. Each error should be evaluated in
light of its effect on an operation.

A Program of Inspection

Inspections are non-productive actions; therefore, whenever
an inspection can be eliminated or combined, a process will have
been simplified and decision making reduced.

The purpose of inspections is to reduce errors. There are
many different possible causes of errors. Errors may be caused
by placing an unqualified person into a position. This applies to
over-qualified as well as under-qualified individuals. Interviewing,
aptitude tests, and other selection techniques have been devised to
minimize improper placement. Errors may also be caused by sub-
standard working conditions. Poor lighting, or ventilation can be
serious detriments to quality work, as can an environment that is
distracting to work. Overcrowded working conditions in processing
divisions can be a cause of errors.

Errors may be due to improper training and supervision.
Efforts should be concentrated from the outset to insure that a new
employee is given adequate opportunity to learn his new job. A
worker who is only half sure of what is expected of him, or has
not been told what to be on the lookout for, is bound to allow errors to pass undetected. Persons responsible for training often
find it difficult to play the role of the beginner; as a result they
take too much for granted regarding the learner's experience and
ability to learn. Often for the sake of expediency, caused by day
to day pressures, training is restricted to explanations of how instead of why.

In spite of all efforts to eliminate inspections, there will
still remain some jobs that require them. Checking work can
either be performed by the same person who performed the work

originally, or by a second person. If it is extremely important
that a high degree of accuracy be maintained, a special inspection
team can be organized.

The inspection process can proceed in either of two general
ways. All work can be reviewed. In this case all that remains is
to decide what types of errors will be tolerated and what errors
will be rejected. A second possible procedure is to employ acceptance sampling. Take for example a group of cards filed in the
catalog. The library decides that it will accept no more than one
per cent error in filing. After the cards are filed, a reviser
checks only a pre-determined random sample. If the sample meets
standards then the remaining work is accepted as satisfactory; but
if the sample proves to be sub-standard an additional check could
be made (the larger the sample, the greater its reliability -- See
Chapter VIII). If the filer's work proved to be sub-standard then
all of the filing would have to be revised, and remedial action initiated later. The technique for developing an acceptance sampling
program is discussed thoroughly in many basic statistics books.

Feedback

If a job warrants inspection, then the information gleaned
from the inspection should be used as feedback to the person who
performed the original work or his supervisor. Corrective action
such as additional training might be in order. If a worker has
simply been careless or lax and this becomes a chronic occurrence
then some harsher action may be necessary. Feedback is an essential feature of an inspection program. Without it an inspection
program looses a substantial part of its effectiveness.

Notes

1. Henry Voos, "Standard Times for Certain Clerical Activities in
   Technical Processing" (Ph. D dissertation, Graduate School
   of Library Service, Rutgers, the State University, New
   Brunswick, New Jersey), p. 6.

2. Ibid. , p. 98.

Bibliography
General

Lazarro, Victor, ed.   Systems and Procedures.   Englewood Cliffs,
    N. J. :   Prentice-Hall, 1959.   Chapter 7, 'Work Measure-
    ment. "

Littlefield, Cleatice L. , and Rachel, Frank.   Office and Adminis-
    trative Management.   2nd ed.   Englewood Cliffs, N.J. :
    Prentice-Hall, 1964.   Section 7, "Performance Standards
    and Control. "

Nadler, Gerald.   Work Simplification.   New York, McGraw-Hill,
    1957.   Chapter 17, "Fundamentals of Work Measurement. "

Libraries
Duyvis, Frits D.   "Standardization as a Tool of Scientific Manage-
    ment, "   Library Trends, II, No. 3 (January, 1954), p. 410-
    27.

Shaw, Ralph R.   "Scientific Management in the Library, "   Wilson
    Library Bulletin, XXI, No. 5 (January, 1947), p. 349-57.

Voos, Henry.   Standard Times for Certain Clerical Activities in
    Technical Processing.   (Ph. D dissertation.   Rutgers, the
    State University, 1964.)   Available from University Micro-
    films.

Chapter XII
Study of A Circulation System
-- the Present Method

In the preceding chapters we have presented the fundamentals of flow process charting, time study, and cost analysis. Particular emphasis has been placed on these techniques. They are the basic tools of the system analyst. To illustrate how these basic techniques can be applied, a study of a circulation system of a public library will be presented.

Setting the Stage

The library we are to study is located in an industrial community of slightly more than 40,000 people. The community is library oriented, and as a result, the library has been well supported. This community, like most in our country, is on the threshold of a student enrollment explosion. Demands for reference service and circulation are spiraling upward. To insure that city funds are spent as judiciously as possible and in order to meet new demands for service, the librarian has requested a survey of the library's circulation system and recommendations for improvement in the procedures and policies that govern it. The librarian has also requested that we calculate the unit cost for circulating a book.

The Preliminary Steps

The minimum acceptable service objectives must first be defined clearly. We can formulate these through interviews with the library board, the head librarian, and other staff members. This indicates that the library will be satisfied as long as it can identify each item borrowed and the person who borrowed it when the library is ready to recall overdue items. The library is using a numerical-time control circulation system, more commonly known as a transaction card system, which satisfactorily provides this type of control.

182

Constructing a Block Diagram

The block diagram will prove useful in defining the limits
of the circulation system.   All routines associated with circulation
are included in the block diagram in order to make sure that the
entire cycle of the charging system is covered by the study.   For
a block diagram of the circulation system, see Figure 12-1.

The book preparation routine, which includes the operations
of pasting the book pockets and typing information on the book
cards has been included as part of the circulation system.   In some
studies, the costs incurred in these procedures are charged to
processing rather than circulation.   However, we have decided to
assign these costs to circulation because they are performed only
on books destined to circulate.

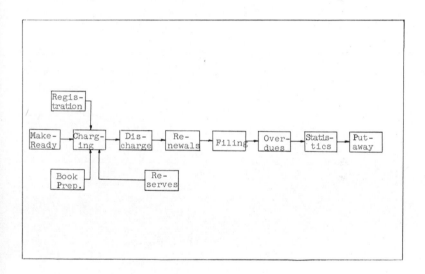

Fig. 12-1 Block diagram of the circulation system.

The floor layout shows the areas where circulation work is
performed.   (See Figure 12-2).   These include the circulation desk,
the main floor workroom, the cataloging room (2nd floor), the reference room, and what is usually termed the readers' adviser
area.   There are some book stacks located around the perimeters

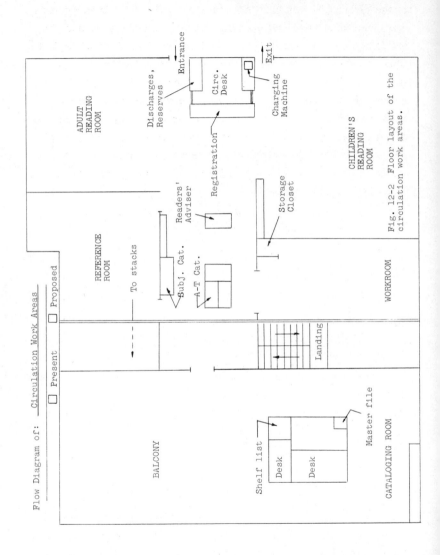

Flow Diagram of: __Circulation Work Areas__

☐ Present   ☐ Proposed

Fig. 12-2 Floor layout of the circulation work areas.

of the reading rooms, but the main stacks are on the main floor directly beneath the balcony.   The figure has not been drawn to scale, but the general spatial relationships have been retained.

Brief Description of the Circulation Desk Work Area

The circulation desk work area is shown in Figure 12-3. It is in this area that most of the work that will be described is performed.   The desk is situated centrally between the public entrance and exit.   This arrangement not only makes possible a maximum of control but also allows minimum staffing during slack hours.

Fig. 12-3 Circulation desk area

Constructing the Flow Process Charts

We are now ready to prepare a flow process chart (and flow diagram when needed) for each procedure. With our forms, pencils, and eraser grasped firmly, we venture forth.

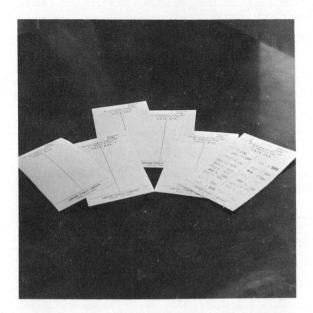

Fig. 12-4

Fig. 12-5

FLOW PROCESS CHART					SUMMARY		
					Pres. Meth.	Prop. Meth.	Diff.
Subject Charted: __Make-Ready Procedures__							
Present [X] or Proposed [ ] Method Type of Chart [X] Man [ ] Product				Operations			
Chart Begins: __Opens safe__				Transportations			
Chart Ends: __Puts away ink pad__				Inspections			
Charted By: __R. Smith__ Date: __3/31/1966__ Sheet __1__ of __2__				Delays			
				Distance in feet			

Dist. in feet	Time in Min.	Symbol	Step no.	Description of Event
				GETTING THE CASH DRAWER FROM SAFE
		○	1.	Opens safe.
		○	2.	Removes cash drawer from safe.
42		⇨	3.	To circulation desk.
		○	4.	Dates fine money tally slip.
		○	5.	Places cash tray in desk.
				NOTE: This routine is performed once each working day.
				CHANGING DATE ON FILM
6		⇨	1.	To charging machine.
		○	2.	Writes current date on a scratch card.
		○	3.	Turns on charging machine.
		○	4.	Inserts scratch card.
		○	5.	Pulls card from tray.
		○	6.	Throws scratch card away.
		○	7.	Turns off machine.
				STAMPING DATE DUE ON TRANSACTION CARDS (Fig. 12-4).
		○	1.	Removes stack of undated transaction cards, T-cards, from tray.
		○	2.	Opens ink pad.
		○	3.	Picks up dater.
		⇨	4.	Inspects for correct date.
		○	5.	Dates T-cards (Fig. 12-5).
		○	6.	Returns dated stack of T-cards to tray.
		○	7.	Places dater on desk.
		○	8.	Puts away ink pad.

FLOW PROCESS CHART					SUMMARY			
						Pres. Meth.	Prop. Meth.	Diff.
Subject Charted: _Make-ready Procedures_					Operations	17		
Present ☒ or Proposed ☐ Method │ Type of Chart ☒ Man ☐ Product					Transpor- tations	2		
Chart Begins: _Opens safe._					Inspections	1		
Chart Ends: _Puts away ink pad._					Delays			
Charted By: _R. Smith_ Date: _3/31/1966_ Sheet _2_ of _2_					Distance in feet	48		

Dist. in feet	Time in Min.	Symbol	Step no.	Description of Event
				NOTE: This routine can be performed daily or weekly depending on the size of the library and its circulation. In the library we are studying, it is performed once each week. Other libraries purchase pre-dated, disposable T-cards that are discarded after one use.

Fig. 12-6

Fig. 12-7

				FLOW PROCESS CHART	SUMMARY		

FLOW PROCESS CHART

SUMMARY

Subject Charted: Preparation of books for circulation.

Present [X] or Proposed [ ] Method | Type of Chart [X] Man [ ] Product

Chart Begins: To closet from work desk.

Chart Ends: Transports book truck to reader adviser's desk.

Charted By: R. Smith Date: 3/31/1966 Sheet 1 of 2

		Pres. Meth.	Prop. Meth.	Diff.
Operations				
Transportations				
Inspections				
Delays				
Distance in feet				

Dist. in feet	Time in Min.	Symbol	Step no.	Description of Event
10			1.	To closet from work desk.
			2.	Picks up book slips, book pockets, plastic jackets, and glue.
10			3.	To desk.
			4.	Sits down.
			5.	Picks up first book.
			6.	Opens book.
			7.	Removes order card.
			8.	Inspects book.
				NOTE: No cards are typed for reference books.
			9.	Inserts book pocket and book slip into typewriter (Fig. 12-6).
			10.	Types following information on cards: call number, if non-fiction, author's surname, short title, date of publication, and price plus $.25 for processing.
			11.	Removes cards from machine.
			12.	Picks up accession stamp(Fig. 12-7).
				NOTE: A Bates Numbering Machine.
			13.	Stamps accession number on book slip.
			14.	Stamps number on book pocket.
			15.	Stamps number on verso of title page.
				NOTE: The accession numbers are being used in place of copy numbers, that is, their two functions are to distinguish between different copies of the same title, and to provide the library with a count of volumes added.

	FLOW PROCESS CHART			SUMMARY		

Subject Charted: **Preparation of books for circulation.**

Present [X] or Proposed [ ] Method | Type of Chart [X] Man [ ] Product

Chart Begins: __To closet from work desk.__

Chart Ends: __Transports truck to reader adviser's desk.__

Charted By: __R. Smith__ Date: __3/31/1966__ Sheet __2__ of __2__

				Pres. Meth.	Prop. Meth.	Diff.
Operations				18		
Transportations				5		
Inspections				1		
Delays						
Distance in feet				60		

Dist. in feet	Time in Min.	Symbol	Step no.	Description of Event
		○	16.	Places accession stamp on desk.
		○	17.	Glues book pocket into book (Fig. 12-8).
		○	18.	Places plastic jacket on all books having dust jackets (Fig. 12-9).
			19.	Closes book.
			20.	Places book on book truck.
				NOTE: Steps five through twenty are repeated until all books are prepared. From now on all repeated steps will be bracketed by a "re-cycle" arrow.
10		⇨	21.	To closet.
		○	22.	Puts away unused supplies.
10		⇨	23.	To work station.
20		⇨	24.	Transports book truck to reader adviser's desk.

Fig. 12-8

Fig. 12-9

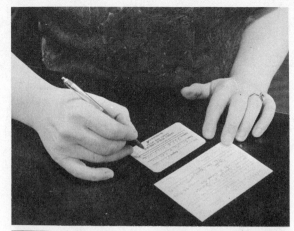

Fig. 12-10

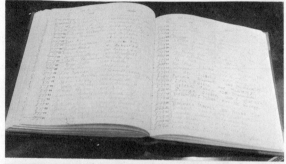

Fig. 12-11

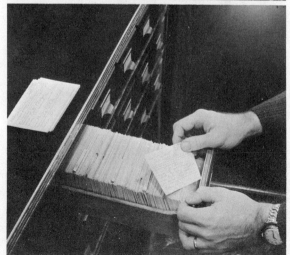

Fig. 12-12

FLOW PROCESS CHART					SUMMARY		
					Pres. Meth.	Prop. Meth.	Diff.
Subject Charted: Registration of new borrowers							
Present [X] or Proposed [ ] Method Type of Chart [X] Man [ ] Product				Operations			
Chart Begins: Greets prospective borrower.				Transportations			
Chart Ends: Files card.				Inspections			
Charted By: R. Smith Date: 4/1/1966 Sheet 1 of 2				Delays			
				Distance in feet			

Dist. in feet	Time in Min.	Symbol	Step no.	Description of Event
		○	1.	Greets prospective borrower.
		○	2.	Asks borrower's name.
		□	3.	Examines master registration file.
				NOTE: This performed so that those who already owe the library money will not be issued a new library card.
		○	4.	Asks borrower for identification.
		□	5.	Examines identification.
				NOTE: This is to establish residency. If a prospective borrower cannot produce some identification, a library card will not be issued.
		○	6.	Gives an application form to borrower.
		○	7.	Picks up a borrower's card.
		○	8.	Stamps expiration date on borrower's card.
		○	9.	Opens numerical registration book.
		▽	10.	Waits for borrower to complete application form.
		○	11.	Receives registration card from borrower.
		□	12.	Inspects card for completeness of information.
		○	13.	Fills out reader's library card (Fig. 12-10).
		○	14.	Records borrower's name and address in numerical registration book (Fig. 12-11).
		○	15.	Hands reader his new library card.

FLOW PROCESS CHART				SUMMARY		

Subject Charted: __Registration of new borrowers.__

Present [X] or Proposed [ ] Method   Type of Chart [X] Man [ ] Product

Chart Begins: __Greets prospective borrower.__

Chart Ends: __Files card.__

Charted By: __R. Smith__ Date: __4/1/1966__ Sheet __2__ of __2__

	Pres. Meth.	Prop. Meth.	Diff.
Operations	19		
Transpor- tations	3		
Inspections	3		
Delays	1		
Distance in feet	27		

Dist. in feet	Time in Min.	Symbol	Step no.	Description of Event
		◯	16.	Copies registration number on registration application.
		◯	17.	Closes numerical registration book.
		◯	18.	Prints borrower's name along top edge of application form. NOTE: This is done to facilitate filing later.
12		⇨	19.	To reader adviser's desk.
		◯	20.	Introduces new reader to the librarian on duty.
12		⇨	21.	To circulation desk.
		◯	22.	Drops application card into tray for filing later.
				FILING NEW REGISTRATION CARDS INTO ALPHABETICAL FILE
		◯	1.	Removes registration cards from holding tray.
		◯	2.	Alphabetizes cards by borrower name.
3		⇨	3.	To registration file.
		◯	4.	Files cards (Fig. 12-12).

Fig. 12-13

Fig. 12-14

Fig. 12-15

Fig. 12-16

FLOW PROCESS CHART					SUMMARY		
					Pres. Meth.	Prop. Meth.	Diff.
Subject Charted: Charging out materials.				Operations			
Present [X] or Proposed [ ] Method	Type of Chart [X] Man [ ] Product			Transpor- tations			
Chart Begins: Turns on charging machine.				Inspections			
Chart Ends: Returns card to patron.				Delays			
Charted By: R. Smith Date: 4/1-2/1966 Sheet 1 of 2				Distance in feet			

Dist. in feet	Time in Min.	Symbol	Step no.	Description of Event
				CHARGING OUT FIRST BOOK
			1.	Turns on charging machine.
			2.	Asks for (or accepts) reader's library card (Fig. 12-13).
			3.	Inspects reader's card.
			4.	Opens book.
			5.	Inserts reader's card into machine. (Fig. 12-14).
			6.	Removes top T-card from pile (Fig. 12-15).
			7.	Inserts T-card into machine.
			8.	Pulls book slip from book.
			9.	Inserts book slip into machine.
			10.	Picks up T-card and book slip from machine (Fig. 12-16).
			11.	Inserts book slip and T-card into book pocket.
			12.	Picks up borrower's card from machine.
			13.	Returns card to patron.
			14.	Closes books.
				NOTE: This procedure is followed when only one item is charged.
				CHARGING OUT SECOND BOOK
			1.	Pulls T-card from pile of cards.
			2.	Inserts T-card into machine.
			3.	Opens book.
			4.	Pulls book slip from book pocket.
			5.	Inserts book slip into machine.
			6.	Turns off machine.

FLOW PROCESS CHART			SUMMARY			
				Pres. Meth.	Prop. Meth.	Diff.
Subject Charted: Charging out materials			Operations	24		
Present [X] or Proposed [ ] Method Type of Chart [X] Man [ ] Product			Transpor- tations			
Chart Begins: Turns on charging machine.			Inspections	1		
Chart Ends: Returns card to patron.			Delays			
Charted By: R. Smith Date: 4/1-2/1966 Sheet 2 of 2			Distance in feet			

Dist. in feet	Time in Min.	Symbol	Step no.	Description of Event
		○	7.	Picks up T-card and book slip from tray.
		○	8.	Places book slip and T-card into book pocket.
		○	9.	Closes book.
		○	10.	Picks up borrower's card from machine.
		○	11.	Returns card to patron.

Fig. 12-17

Fig. 12-18

Fig. 12-19

Fig. 12-20

FLOW PROCESS CHART

	SUMMARY			
		Pres. Meth.	Prop. Meth.	Diff.
Subject Charted: _Discharging books and collecting overdue fines._				
	Operations	12		
Present [X] or Proposed [ ] Method Type of Chart [X] Man [ ] Product	Transpor-tations	2		
Chart Begins: _Accepts book from reader._				
Chart Ends: _To discharging point._	Inspections	1		
	Delays			
Charted By: _R. Smith_ Date: _4/4/1966_ Sheet _1_ of _1_	Distance in feet	12		

Dist. in feet	Time in Min.	Symbol	Step no.	Description of Event
		○	1.	Accepts book(s) from reader.
		○	2.	Opens book to expose T-card.
		□	3.	Inspect T-card to see if book is overdue (Fig. 12-17).
		○	4.	Places T-card into return file.
		○	5.	Checks book against the reserve file.
		○	6.	Places book on truck for shelving.
				COLLECTING FINES FOR OVERDUE BOOKS
		○	1.	Calculates amount of money owed (Fig. 12-18).
		○	2.	Collects fine money from reader.
		○	3.	Places fine money into cash drawer.
		○	4.	Records amount of fine collected on a tally sheet (Fig. 12-19).
				NOTE: Children are not charged fines in this library.
				IF READER IS UNABLE TO PAY FINE
		○	1.	Desk attendant locates scratch card.
		○	2.	Fills in the following information: identity of the borrower, amount owed, reason for debt, and date (Fig. 12-20).
6		⇨	3.	To registration file.
		○	4.	Attaches slip to borrower's registration card.
6		⇨	5.	Returns to discharging point.

Flow Diagram of: Reserve procedure

▣ Present   □ Proposed

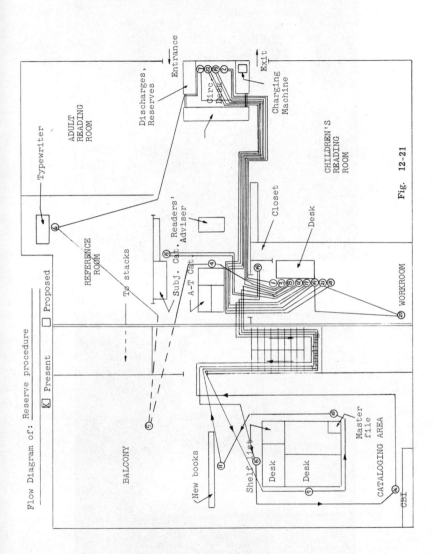

ADULT READING ROOM

Typewriter

Entrance

Discharges, Reserves

Circ. Desk

Exit

Charging Machine

REFERENCE ROOM

To stacks

Readers' Adviser

Subj. Cat.

A-T Cat.

Closet

Desk

CHILDREN'S READING ROOM

WORKROOM

BALCONY

New books

Shelf list

Desk

Desk

Master file

CATALOGING AREA

OBI

Fig. 12-21

Fig. 12-22

Fig. 12-23

FLOW PROCESS CHART

			SUMMARY			
Subject Charted: Processing reserves.				Pres. Meth.	Prop. Meth.	Diff.
Present [X] or Proposed [ ] Method Type of Chart [X] Man [ ] Product			Operations			
Chart Begins: To circulation desk from workroom.			Transpor- tations			
Chart Ends: Files card in NCF file.			Inspections			
Charted By: R. Smith Date: 4/5-6/1965 Sheet 1 of 4			Delays			
			Distance in feet			

Dist. in feet	Time in Min.	Symbol	Step no.	Description of Event
				(For flow diagram of reserve processing, see Fig. 12-21).
42			1.	To circulation desk from workroom.
			2.	Picks up accumulation of reserve applications.
42			3.	To workroom.
			4.	Arranges requests into alphabetical order by author of title requested.
			5.	Dates reserves if not already dated.
				NOTE: Date fixes order of priority.
			6.	Checks reserve file to see if the title is already on reserve (Fig. 12-22).
			7.	Places request with other request(s).
				IF TITLE IS NOT CURRENTLY ON RESERVE
15			1.	To card catalog.
			2.	Checks author-title catalog to learn if the library owns the book requested.
300			3.	To shelves to learn if book(s) is currently in the library.
			4.	Checks shelf for book.
				NOTE: If book is located, it is processed for reserve.
60			5.	To typewriter.
			6.	Types a strip for the visible file for each title.
50			7.	To the circulation desk.
			8.	Inserts strips into visible file (Fig. 12-23).
42			9.	To workroom.

FLOW PROCESS CHART				SUMMARY		
					Pres. Meth.	Prop. Meth.	Diff.

Subject Charted: __Processing reserves.__

				Operations			
Present [X] or Proposed [ ] Method	Type of Chart [X] Man [ ] Product	Transportations			
Chart Begins: __To circulation desk from workroom.__					
Chart Ends: __Files card in NCF file.__				Inspections			
				Delays			
Charted By: __R. Smith__ Date: _4/5-6/1966_ Sheet _2_ of _4_				Distance in feet			

Dist. in feet	Time in Min.	Symbol	Step no.	Description of Event
				IF LIBRARY HAS NOT CATALOGED TITLE REQUESTED
62			1.	To upstairs cataloging room.
			2.	Searches outstanding order file.
			3.	Searches L. C. card file.
14			4.	To master file.
			5.	Searches the master file.
				NOTE: Master file is an inventory of books received during the past twenty-four months.
			6.	Notes on reserve card that book requested is on order.
				NOTE: Whenever a title is found to be on order, reservation is noted by flagging the order card.
				IF A REQUESTED TITLE IS CURRENTLY BEING PROCESSED
10			1.	To shelves with books being cataloged.
			2.	Searches for requested titles.
10			3.	To cataloger's desk.
			4.	Inserts yellow strip into book.
			5.	Places book on desk for RUSH processing.
62			6.	To workroom.
			7.	Files reserve requests.
				IF A BOOK IS NEITHER OWNED NOR ON ORDER
16			1.	To bookcase where __BIP__ is located.
			2.	Searches __BIP__ for biblio. information.
16			3.	To workroom.
			4.	Searches __Virginia Kirkus__.

		FLOW PROCESS CHART			SUMMARY		
					Pres. Meth.	Prop. Meth.	Diff.
Subject Charted: _Processing reserves._				Operations			
Present [X] or Proposed [ ] Method	Type of Chart [X] Man [ ] Product			Transpor- tations			
Chart Begins: _To circulation desk from workroom._				Inspections			
Chart Ends: _Files card in NCF file._				Delays			
Charted By: _R. Smith_ Date: _4/5-6/1966_ Sheet _3_ of _4_				Distance in feet			

Dist. in feet	Time in Min.	Symbol	Step no.	Description of Event
62			5.	To upstairs cataloging room.
			6.	Searches <u>Publisher's Weekly</u>.
			7.	Searches <u>Cumulative Book Index</u>.
75			8.	To downstairs workroom.
			9.	Places completed work in consideration file for Librarian's attention.
				NOTE: Whenever necessary biblio- graphical information is located the procedure is ended. The actual study was traced through a number of requests in order to determine the percentage of requests pinpointed by each sub-procedure. The times and costs reflect the various frequencies of occurrence. One method for clearly distinguish- ing between sub-routines is to use the flow decision chart as des- cribed in Chapter IV.
				PREPARING RESERVED BOOKS FOR CIRCULATION
42			1.	To the circulation desk.
			2.	Gathers titles.
				NOTE: Reserved titles are set aside when a desk attendant dis- covers that a title has been re- quested (See Discharging Procedure).
42			3.	To workroom.
			4.	Takes drawer of reserve requests from cabinet.
			5.	Pulls request card from file.
			6.	Places card on desk.
			7.	Writes patron's name and time book will be held.

FLOW PROCESS CHART					SUMMARY		
					Pres. Meth.	Prop. Meth.	Diff.
Subject Charted: Processing reserves.				Operations	37		
Present [X] or Proposed [ ] Method	Type of Chart [X] Man [ ] Product			Transpor- tations	22		
Chart Begins: To circulation desk from workroom.				Inspections			
Chart Ends: Files card in NCF file.				Delays			
Charted By: R. Smith Date: 4/5-6/1966 Sheet 4 of 4				Distance in feet	1066		

Dist. in feet	Time in Min.	Symbol	Step no.	Description of Event
		○	8.	Places card into book.
		○	9.	Fills out reserve notice to be sent to reader (Fig. 12-24).
		○	10.	Places stamp on card.
10		⇨	11.	To mailbox.
		○	12.	Places postal into mailbox.
10		⇨	13.	To desk.
		○	14.	Arranges books alphabetically by reader's name.
42		⇨	15.	To the circulation desk.
		○	16.	Inter-files books with other reserved titles awaiting patron pick-up (Fig. 12-25).
				PROCESSING "NOT CALLED FOR" RESERVES
				NOTE: Occasionally a reader will fail to pick-up a book he had previously requested.
		○	1.	Removes books from the "reserve shelf."
42		⇨	2.	To workroom.
		○	3.	Pulls scratch card from book.
		○	4.	Writes author, title, current date, and NCF, Not Circulated File, on card.
		○	5.	Files card in NCF file.
				NOTE: At this point, the books would either be returned to the shelves or put back into the reserve procedure, if there were another request for the title.

Fig. 12-24

Fig. 12-25

Fig.
12-26

Fig.
12-27

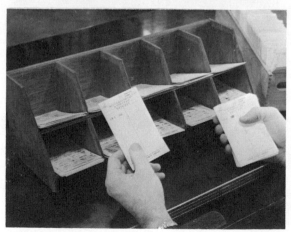

Fig.
12-28

<table>
<tr><td colspan="2">FLOW PROCESS CHART</td><td colspan="4">SUMMARY</td></tr>
</table>

FLOW PROCESS CHART		SUMMARY			
Subject Charted: Sorting transaction cards.			Pres. Meth.	Prop. Meth.	Diff.
		Operations	5		
Present [X] or Proposed [ ] Method	Type of Chart [X] Man [ ] Product	Transpor- tations	2		
Chart Begins: Stacks T-cards as they are received.					
Chart Ends: To circulation desk.		Inspections			
		Delays			
Charted By: R. Smith Date: 4/6/1966 Sheet 1 of 1		Distance in feet	84		

Dist. in feet	Time in Min.	Symbol	Step no.	Description of Event
		○	1.	Stacks T-cards as they are received.
		○	2.	Rough sorts cards by series (Fig. 12-26).
		○	3.	Rough sorts cards by hundreds within series.
		○	4.	Interfiles cards with other discharged T-cards within a series (Fig. 12-27).
				NOTE: The library we are investigating employees thirteen separate series of T-cards. Each series is used for times each year. The interval of three months is intended to allow sufficient time for all outstanding cards to be returned. If a card is not returned, a substitute card is prepared; the same procedure is followed whenever a reader loses a T-card.
42		⇨	5.	To mainfloor workroom.
		○	6.	Interfiles preceding day's returned T-cards into the master file (Fig. 12-28).
42		⇨	7.	To circulation desk.
				NOTE: The interfiling is usually performed once a day.

Flow Diagram of: Overdues Procedure

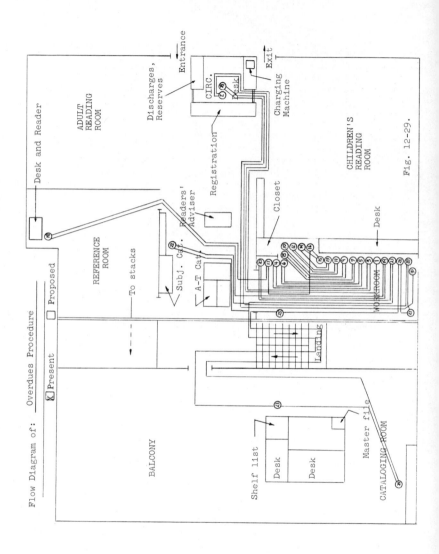

Fig. 12-29.

Fig. 12-30

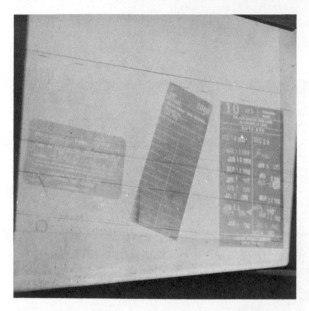

Fig. 12-31

Fig. 12-32

FLOW PROCESS CHART

Subject Charted: Processing overdue notices.

Present [X] or Proposed [ ]   Method   Type of Chart [X] Man [ ] Product

Chart Begins: __ To circulation desk from workroom.

Chart Ends: __ To workroom.

Charted By: __ R. Smith __ Date: 4/13-15/66 __ Sheet 1 of 4

	SUMMARY		
	Pres. Meth.	Prop. Meth.	Diff.
Operations			
Transportations			
Inspections			
Delays			
Distance in feet			

Dist. in feet	Time in Min.	Symbol	Step no.	Description of Event
				(For a flow diagram of the overdues procedure, see Fig. 12-29).
42			1.	To circulation desk from workroom.
			2.	Picks up notebook used to record T-nos.
			3.	Empties box of T-cards for books overdue three weeks or more.
42			4.	To main floor workroom.
			5.	Places notebook and T-cards on desk.
24(8x3)			6.	To T-card storage area.
			7.	Picks up tray of T-cards.
24(8x3)			8.	To desk.
				NOTE: Steps six through eight are repeated twice.
			9.	Sorts through cards (card by card).
			10.	Writes T-numbers of all missing cards in notebook (Fig. 12-30).
				NOTE: These numbers represent books that have not been returned to the library.
24(8x3)			11.	To T-card storage area.
			12.	Places tray of T-cards in cabinet.
24(8x3)			13.	To desk.
				NOTE: Steps eleven through thirteen are repeated twice.
3			14.	To T-card storage area (carries notebook and pencil).
			15.	Replaces last tray of T-cards.
6			16.	To microfilm cabinet.
			17.	Selects appropriate roll of microfilm.
58			18.	To microfilm reader located in Reference room.

FLOW PROCESS CHART

	SUMMARY		
	Pres. Meth.	Prop. Meth.	Diff.
Operations			
Transpor-tations			
Inspections			
Delays			
Distance in feet			

Subject Charted: __Processing overdue notices.__

Present [X] or Proposed [ ] Method   Type of Chart [X] Man [ ] Product

Chart Begins: __To circulation desk from workroom.__

Chart Ends: __To workroom.__

Charted By: __R. Smith__ Date: __4/13-15/66__ Sheet __2__ of __4__

Dist. in feet	Time in Min.	Symbol	Step no.	Description of Event
			19.	Threads film into reader.
			20.	Turns on machine.
			21.	Checks pad for first T-number.
			22.	Searches for corresponding T-number on film (Fig. 12-31).
			23.	Types overdue notice (Fig. 12-32). NOTE: Four part fanfolds are used first.
			24.	Records date overdue notice was prepared in notebook.
			25.	Rewinds film.
			26.	Turns off machine.
			27.	Removes film from machine.
58			28.	To workroom desk with overdue notices.
			29.	Places work on desk.
8			30.	To microfilm cabinet with film.
			31.	Returns film to cabinet.
8			32.	To desk.
			33.	Checks "Red Card" or "Snag" file. NOTE: Whenever a book is returned without a T-card in it, a temporary T-card is prepared. Included on the card are a bibliographic citation for the material and the identity of the borrower.

SEARCHING FOR BOOK PRICE INFORMATION WHEN NOT FOUND ON FILM

Dist. in feet	Time in Min.	Symbol	Step no.	Description of Event
16			34.	To area where BIP is stored.
			35.	Checks BIP for price.
62			36.	To upstairs workroom.
			37.	Checks shelflist for price.
13			38.	To area where CBI is shelved.

				FLOW PROCESS CHART	SUMMARY		
						Pres. Meth.	Prop. Meth.	Diff.

Subject Charted: **Processing overdue notices.**

Present ☒ or Proposed ☐ Method Type of Chart ☒ Man ☐ Product

Chart Begins: **To circulation desk from workroom.**

Chart Ends: **To workroom.**

Charted By: **R. Smith** Date: **4/13-15/66** Sheet **3** of **4**

					Pres. Meth.	Prop. Meth.	Diff.
Operations							
Transportations							
Inspections							
Delays							
Distance in feet							

Dist. in feet	Time in Min.	Symbol	Step no.	Description of Event
			39.	Checks CBI for price.
68			40.	To main floor workroom.
			41.	Gathers envelopes and stamps from safe.
8			42.	To desk.
			43.	Checks recently returned overdue T-cards against numbers listed in notebook.
				NOTE: This operation is performed in order to avoid sending patrons notices who have just returned their overdue books.
			44.	Removes throw-away carbons from overdue notices(Fig. 12-33).
			45.	Tears off top copy of fanfold.
			46.	Folds form in half.
			47.	Stuffs notice into window envelope (Fig. 12-34).
			48.	Stamps envelope.
			49.	Seals envelope.
18			50.	To mailbox.
			51.	Drops notices into box.
18			52.	To work area.
			53.	Picks up remaining copies of notices.
42			54.	To circulation desk.
			55.	Files notices.
42			56.	To workroom.
				SECOND NOTICE
42			1.	To circulation desk.
			2.	Picks up last week's notices (Fig. 12-35).
42			3.	To workroom.
			4.	Checks notices against recently returned overdue T-cards.

FLOW PROCESS CHART					SUMMARY		
					Pres. Meth.	Prop. Meth.	Diff.
Subject Charted: Processing overdue notices.							
				Operations	57		
Present X or Proposed ☐ Method Type of Chart X Man ☐ Product				Transpor- tations	33		
Chart Begins: To circulation desk from workroom.							
				Inspections			
Chart Ends: To workroom.							
				Delays			
Charted By: R. Smith Date: 4/13-15/66 Sheet 4 of 4				Distance in feet	1008		

Dist. in feet	Time in Min.	Symbol	Step no.	Description of Event
		◯	5.	Checks "red card" file.
			6-17.	Repeats steps 45-56 above.
				THIRD NOTICE
42		⇨	1.	To circulation desk.
		◯	2.	Locates last week's second notices and deliquent notices.
42		⇨	3.	To workroom.
		◯	4.	Checks against recently returned overdue T-cards.
		◯	5.	Checks "red card" file.
			6-15.	Repeats steps 45-54 above.
		◯	16.	Files remaining notices into the delinquent file.
42		⇨	17.	To workroom.
				NOTE: The procedure employed to process delinquent notices is, for the most part, non-repetitive. The action taken depends on the circumstances in each case. The primary management considerations would be to insure that the library's governing policies were practical and necessary.

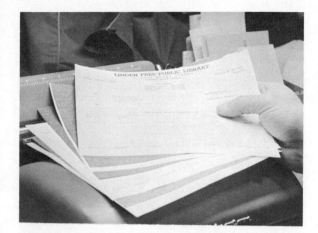

Fig. 12-33

Fig. 12-34

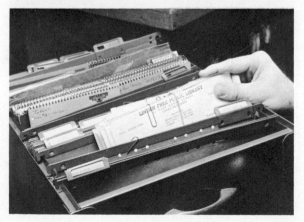

Fig. 12-35

FLOW PROCESS CHART				SUMMARY			
					Pres. Meth.	Prop. Meth.	Diff.
Subject Charted: _Processing renewals._							
				Operations	6		
Present [X] or Proposed [ ] Method	Type of Chart [X] Man [ ] Product			Transpor- tations			
Chart Begins: _Answers telephone._							
				Inspections			
Chart Ends: _Replaces receiver._							
				Delays	1		
Charted By: _R. Smith_ Date: _4/10/1966_ Sheet _1_ of _1_				Distance in feet			

Dist. in feet	Time in Min.	Symbol	Step no.	Description of Event
				NOTE: If a renewal request is made in person, the transaction is handled as a new loan.
		◯	1.	Answers telephone.
		▽	2.	Listens to reader's request.
		◯	3.	Checks to learn if book is on reserve.
		◯	4.	Fills out dummy, red T-card (Fig. 12-36).
				NOTE: The following information is recorded: the T-number, date due, author and title, and the borrower's name and address. The card if filed in its regular sequence. However, when overdue notices for this series are prepared, none will be sent for the renewed title.
		◯	5.	Places T-card in with other T-cards for discharged books.
		◯	6.	Informs reader when renewed book will be due.
		◯	7.	Replaces receiver.

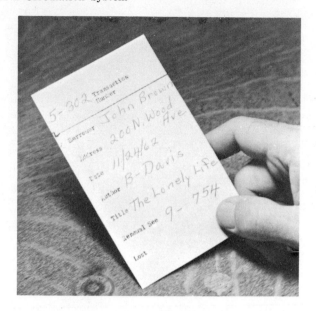

Fig. 12-36

Fig. 12-37

FLOW PROCESS CHART		SUMMARY			

Subject Charted: Recording circulation statistics.

	Pres. Meth.	Prop. Meth.	Diff.
Operations	4		
Transportations	2		
Inspections			
Delays			
Distance in feet	12		

Present [X] or Proposed [ ] Method   Type of Chart [X] Man [ ] Product

Chart Begins: Picks up circulation statistics book.

Chart Ends: Returns statistic book to desk.

Charted By: R. Smith   Date: 4/12/1966 Sheet 1 of 1

Dist. in feet	Time in Min.	Symbol	Step no.	Description of Event
		◯	1.	Picks up circulation statistics book (Fig. 12-37).
6		⇨	2.	To charging area.
		◯	3.	Checks to determine T-number of last book charged out in a series.
		◯	4.	Records number of books charged during the week in the statistics book.
6		⇨	5.	To registration area.
		◯	6.	Returns statistic book to desk.
				NOTE: The library records only the total number of items borrowed. No distinction is made between adult and juvenile loans. The percentage distribution is ascertained by sampling the film records once a year.

FLOW PROCESS CHART					SUMMARY		
						Pres. Meth.	Prop. Meth.	Diff.

FLOW PROCESS CHART

Subject Charted: __Put-away procedures.__

Present [X] or Proposed [ ] Method   Type of Chart [X] Man [ ] Product

Chart Begins: __Opens cash drawer.__

Chart Ends: __Takes day's fines to Librarian's office.__

Charted By: __R. Smith__ Date: __4/13-14/196__ Sheet __1__ of __1__

SUMMARY

	Pres. Meth.	Prop. Meth.	Diff.
Operations	10		
Transpor- tations	2		
Inspections			
Delays			
Distance in feet	117		

Dist. in feet	Time in Min.	Symbol	Step no.	Description of Event
		◯	1.	Opens cash drawer.
		◯	2.	Picks up cash tray.
		◯	3.	Sits down at desk.
		◯	4.	Counts money.
		◯	5.	Adds total fines recorded on tally slip.
		◯	6.	Reconciles two balances.
		◯	7.	Places change in cash drawer for next day's use.
		◯	8.	Places receipts in cash bag.
42		⇨	9.	To safe with cash tray and bag.
		◯	10.	Places cash drawer in safe.
		◯	11.	Locks safe.
75		⇨	12.	To Librarian's office with fine money.

NOTE: Fine receipts are accumulated until a sufficient amount has been collected. At that time, the money is disposed in the manner prescribed by city ordinance.

Chapter XIII
Study of A Circulation System
-- the Proposed Method

The most challenging phase of our task is still before us. Even with the basic principles as guides, we will still need plenty of ingenuity and imagination.

The solution we develop will be applicable only for the library we have studied, since, unfortunately, there is still very little standardization among libraries. The ensuing solution should therefore not be regarded as formula to be applied blindly to other situations.

As we develop our proposal, we must keep in mind that a conflict will occasionally arise between the concepts of service and operational efficiency. The goal, once minimum service objectives were established, is to develop those procedures that would guarantee the desired level of services at minimum cost and the most economical approach can only be evaluated in terms of the level of service.

The first step in designing a new system is analysis of the present procedures by posing the six questions: why, what, where, when, who and how. Particular attention should be paid to the procedures which promise the greatest savings in time and effort. (As explained in Chapter II, these are routines requiring frequent movement, high cost operations that are repetitious or are performed frequently, etc.)

Proposed changes are discussed below. This discussion section is then followed by flow process charts and flow diagrams detailing the proposed method. For convenience of the reader, the flow process charts that remain unchanged are repeated in this section. Finally, circulation costs are calculated.

Discussion of the Proposed Method

Make-Ready Procedures

      The make-ready procedures are performed by the circulation desk attendant at the beginning of each day, or, as in the case of dating the transaction cards, once a week. Although we might affect some economy by changing these operations, the resultant savings would be small; therefore, no changes are recommended. (See flow process chart: Make-Ready Procedures.)

Preparation of Books for Circulation

      Present movement will be greatly reduced if supplies are stored at the work station instead of in a closet. It will then only be necessary to replenish supplies periodically.

      At present, an accession number is stamped three times. The purpose of the number is to distinguish between different copies of the same title; therefore, three stampings are unnecessary. One number on the book pocket and one on the book card would be sufficient.

      The author, title, and price (hereafter referred to as the book information) are presently typed on both the book card and the book pocket. The use of two locations is to facilitate filling out a duplicate book card when the original is lost; however, the book information can be found on the title page. Moreover, typing of over 6,000 book pockets per year would be eliminated if this practice were stopped. (See flow process chart: Preparation of Books for Circulation. Here is an example of a procedure which had been designed to accommodate the exception rather than the rule.)

Registration of New Borrowers

      The basic question with regard to registration of new readers is: why? Why maintain both an alphabetical and a numerical record of borrowers or for that matter even one record? What purpose do these records serve? The alphabetical registration file is presently a record of all registered readers, which includes delinquent borrowers. The numerical registration file is a carryover from the days before the library adopted its present circulation system.

Elimination of both registration files will not reduce service
to the public. The library can still retain a file of delinquent borrowers, but for delinquents only. Re-registration can be accom-
modated if necessary by stamping an expiration date prominently on
each reader's library card. Prospective readers will be confronted by less red tape when applying for a library card, and circulation personnel will be able to discard two files. (See flow
process chart: Registration of New Borrowers.)

Charging and Discharging Procedures

Both the charging and discharging procedures appear to be
performed as efficiently as can be expected. It might be possible
to improve them by applying a more sophisticated management tool
such as the operations chart, but the gains would not prove significant because the procedures are not performed continuously.
The benefits derived could not be efficiently utilized; if we saved a
second per book charged, how could we use our new-found time?
Until circulation increases to the point where long lines of patrons
begin to appear during peak borrowing periods, no changes in the
charging and discharging routines are recommended. (See flow
process charts: Charging Out Materials; and Discharging Books
and Collecting Overdue Fines.)

Processing Reserves

Our evaluation of the present reserve procedure shows two
potential avenues for improvement. Procedural changes will produce considerable improvement. Even greater savings would result from two changes in present library policy. But since these
changes would affect service, their merits and possible demerits
will have to be weighed carefully.

Considerable movement would be eliminated if the work station presently used for processing reserves were relocated in the
main floor workroom and if all trade bibliographies were shelved
in a central location. Also, several trips to and from the circulation desk and workroom would be eliminated if work that must be
performed at the circulation desk were batched. These changes

would reduce movement from 1066 to 672 feet, a 37 per cent savings. (See flow process chart: Processing Reserves and Fig. 13-
1).

Whenever a reserve request is for a title the library does
not own, the reserve assistant now searches to determine if the
book is either on order or has been received and is presently being cataloged. This requires a search of three files, one of which
could be eliminated, and the remaining two combined. The "master file" is an inventory of all books ordered and received during
the past couple of years. This file does provide interesting statistics, but its maintenance is not essential. The outstanding order file and the LC card order file could be combined without de-
tracting from their worth. These changes would produce a savings
of approximately 1,500 file searches per year. If a request is received for a title neither owned nor on order, the reserve assistant
attempts to locate bibliographical information for ordering. The
request is then turned over to a librarian for consideration. Since
many titles are not ordered (evaluated as inappropriate, out-of-
print, etc.) it would be more economical to delay the order search
until after the decision to purchase has been made. This would
eliminate approximately half of the present searching.

The number of reserves accepted is increasing significantly.
This growth has not only clogged procedural routines but also
caused service to deteriorate. If the library were to charge a
nickel or dime for each request, the present number of "blanket"
reservations for an entire best seller list, which are now sub-
mitted by some patrons might be reduced. It might also eliminate
some of the borderline requests. The fact that almost 15 per cent
of the processed reserve requests are not picked up by patrons is
a strong indication that many requests spring from short-lived in-
terests.

Sorting Transaction Cards

Examination of the T-card sorting procedure revealed that
the present method was being performed efficiently, but that the
sequence of operations was faulty. The T-cards are sorted on a

day-to-day basis as they are removed from discharged books.
This would be the preferable method if there were any need for the
cards to be arranged prior to preparing the overdue notices, but
this is not the case.

The present work method requires the overdues assistant to
inter-file T-cards into the main file each morning.   Interviews with
the staff indicate that the person now responsible for this work is
barely able to keep up with his work, and as circulation continues
to sky-rocket his plight will worsen.   Observation confirmed this
undesirable situation.

It is recommended that the responsibility for card sorting be
reassigned to circulation desk personnel, and that only one series
of T-cards--the series for which overdue notices are to be made--
be sorted each week just before the overdue notices are prepared.
The work can be performed easily during slack periods, particularly during the morning hours.   These changes will reduce the
time required to sort T-cards by 30 per cent, in addition to re-
lieving the overdues assistant from sorting each morning.   (See
flow process chart: Sorting Transaction Cards).

It is further suggested that when the present supply of T-
cards has been exhausted the library consider the possibility of
substituting disposable cards for the reusable ones now employed.
The costs of the two alternatives should be compared carefully.
Neither type will adversely affect service to the public.

Processing Overdue Notices

The primary problem with overdues work is the excessive
movement from work area to work area.   At present, the assistant
must walk over 2,600 feet per week or over twenty-five miles per
year to perform her job.

It is strongly recommended that all records and tools necessary for processing overdues be relocated in the main floor work
room.   This new rearrangement will reduce movement almost 90
per cent (See Figure 13-3).

Book prices are now searched for if this information is not
found on the book card before the overdue notices are prepared.

Upon examination it was learned that of the 7,500 notices sent during the previous twelve months only in twenty-two cases was the price information actually used. This occurs only when a book is classified "delinquent." Since this information is consulted so seldom, it is suggested that price searches be delayed until after a title is actually declared delinquent (See flow process chart: Processing Overdue Notices).

Renewals

The renewal procedure appears to be as efficient as could be expected.

Recording Circulation Statistics

No recommendations.

Put-Away Procedures

No recommendations.

Summary

If adopted in its entirety the proposed system will eliminate 27 operations, 2 inspections, and 1 delay. Transportations will be reduced from 73 to 34 and the distance traveled reduced from 2,434 to 1,181 feet. This has been summarized in Figure 13-4.

Although by no means the only improvements, three of the most significant gains will come from the elimination of the three files, the reduction of T-card handling time, and the consolidation of the overdues procedure which will eliminate miles of needless walking.

FLOW PROCESS CHART					SUMMARY		
					Pres. Meth.	Prop. Meth.	Diff.
Subject Charted: Make-ready procedures.				Operations	17		
Present ☐ or Proposed ☒ Method Type of Chart ☒ Man ☐ Product				Transpor- tations	2		
Chart Begins: Opens safe.				Inspections	1		
Chart Ends: Puts away ink pad.				Delays			
Charted By: R. Smith Date: 5/1/1966 Sheet 1 of 1				Distance in feet	48		

Dist. in feet	Time in Min.	Symbol	Step no.	Description of Event
				GETTING THE CASH DRAWER FROM THE SAFE
	---		1.	Opens safe.
			2.	Removes cash drawer.
42	1.32		3.	To circulation desk.
			4.	Dates fine money tally slip.
	---		5.	Places cash tray in desk.
				CHANGING DATE ON FILM
6			1.	To charging machine.
			2.	Writes current date on a scratch card.
	.26		3.	Turns on charging machine.
			4.	Inserts scratch card.
			5.	Pulls card from tray.
			6.	Throws scratch card away.
	---		7.	Turns off machine.
				STAMPING DATE DUE ON TRANSACTION CARDS
	---		1.	Removes stack of undated T-cards from tray.
	.16		2.	Opens ink pad.
	---		3.	Picks up dater.
	3.26/100		4.	Inspects for correct date.
			5.	Dates T-cards.
	---		6.	Returns dated stack of T-cards to tray.
	.15		7.	Places dater on desk.
	---		8.	Puts away ink pad.

FLOW PROCESS CHART					SUMMARY			
						Pres. Meth.	Prop. Meth.	Diff.
Subject Charted: Preparation of books for circulation.					Operations	18	14	4
Present ☐ or Proposed ☒ Method	Type of Chart ☒ Man ☐ Product				Transportations	5	1	4
Chart Begins: Picks up first book.					Inspections	1	1	0
Chart Ends: To Reader Adviser's desk with book truck.					Delays			
Charted By: R. Smith Date: 5/2/1966 Sheet 1 of 1					Distance in feet	60	20	40

Dist. in feet	Time in Min.	Symbol	Step no.	Description of Event
	---	○	1.	Picks up first book.
		○	2.	Opens book.
	1.33	○	3.	Removes order card.
		☐	4.	Inspects book.
		○	5.	Inserts book slip into typewriter.
		○	6.	Types book information onto book slip.
		○	7.	Removes slip from typewriter.
	---	○	8.	Picks up accession stamp.
		○	9.	Stamps number on book slip.
	.53	○	10.	Stamps number on book pocket.
	---	○	11.	Places accession stamp on desk.
	1.22	○	12.	Glues book pocket into book.
	---	○	13.	Places plastic jacket on all books with dust jackets.
	2.37	○	14.	Closes book.
	---	○	15.	Shelves book on truck.
20	.27	▷	16.	To Reader Adviser's desk with book truck.

FLOW PROCESS CHART						SUMMARY		
						Pres. Meth.	Prop. Meth.	Diff.
Subject Charted: Registration of new borrowers.					Operations	19	7	12
Present ☐ or Proposed ☒ Method	Type of Chart ☒ Man ☐ Product				Transpor- tations	3	2	1
Chart Begins: Greets prospective borrower.					Inspections	3	2	1
Chart Ends: To desk.					Delays	1	0	1
Charted By: R. Smith Date: 5/3/1966 Sheet 1 of 1					Distance in feet	27	24	3

Dist. in feet	Time in Min.	Symbol	Step no.	Description of Event
	---	○	1.	Greets prospective borrower.
		○	2.	Asks borrower his name.
		☐	3.	Checks delinquent borrower file.
		☐	4.	Asks borrower for some identification.
	1.35	☐	5.	Examines identification.
		○	6.	Fills out reader's library card.
		○	7.	Stamps expiration date at top of card.
		○	8.	Hands card to borrower.
12		○	9.	Takes borrower to Reader Adviser's desk.
		○	10.	Introduces new reader to the librarian on duty.
12	---	▽	11.	To desk.

FLOW PROCESS CHART				SUMMARY			
					Pres. Meth.	Prop. Meth.	Diff.
Subject Charted: Charging out materials.				Operations	24	24	0
Present ☐ or Proposed ☒ Method	Type of Chart ☒ Man ☐ Product			Transpor- tations			
Chart Begins: Turns on charging machine.				Inspections	1	1	0
Chart Ends: Returns card to patron.				Delays			
Charted By: R. Smith Date: 5/4-5/1966 Sheet 1 of 1				Distance in feet			

Dist. in feet	Time in Min.	Symbol	Step no.	Description of Event
				CHARGING OUT FIRST BOOK
---		◯	1.	Turns on charging machine.
		◯	2.	Asks for (or accepts) reader's library card.
		▢	3.	Inspects reader's card.
		◯	4.	Opens book.
		◯	5.	Inserts reader's card into machine.
		◯	6.	Removes top T-card from pile.
	.15	◯	7.	Inserts T-card into machine.
		◯	8.	Pulls book slip from book.
		◯	9.	Inserts book slip into machine.
		◯	10.	Picks up T-card and book slip from machine.
		◯	11.	Inserts book slip and T-card into book pocket.
		◯	12.	Picks up borrower's card from machine.
		◯	13.	Returns card to reader.
---		◯	14.	Closes book.
				CHARGING OUT SECOND BOOK
		◯	1.	Pulls T-card from pile.
		◯	2.	Inserts T-card into machine.
		◯	3.	Opens book.
		◯	4.	Pulls book slip from book pocket.
	.14	◯	5.	Inserts book slip into machine.
		◯	6.	Turns off machine.
		◯	7.	Picks up T-card and book slip from tray.
		◯	8.	Places book slip and T-card into book pocket.
		◯	9.	Closes book.
		◯	10.	Picks up reader's card from machine.
---		◯	11.	Returns card to patron.

FLOW PROCESS CHART			SUMMARY		
				Pres. Meth.	Prop. Meth.	Diff.

FLOW PROCESS CHART				SUMMARY		
Subject Charted: _Discharging books and collecting overdue_ _fines._					Pres. Meth.	Prop. Meth.	Diff.
Present ☐ or Proposed ☒ Method	Type of Chart ☒ Man ☐ Product			Operations	12	12	0
Chart Begins: _Accepts book from reader._				Transpor- tations	2	2	0
Chart Ends: _To discharging area._				Inspections	1	1	0
Charted By: _R. Smith_ Date: _5/6/1966_ Sheet _1_ of _1_				Delays			
				Distance in feet	12	12	0

Dist. in feet	Time in Min.	Symbol	Step no.	Description of Event
		○	1.	Accepts book(s) from reader.
---		○	2.	Opens book to expose T-card.
		○	3.	Inspects T-card to see if book is overdue.
	.10	○	4.	Places T-card into returns pile.
		○	5.	Checks book against the reserve file.
---		○	6.	Places book on truck for shelving.
				COLLECTING FINES FOR OVERDUE BOOKS
		○	1.	Calculates amount of fine.
	.58	○	2.	Collects fine money from borrower.
		○	3.	Places fine money in cash drawer.
---		○	4.	Records fine collected on a tally slip.
				IF READER IS UNABLE TO PAY FINE
		○	1.	Locates a scratch card.
		○	2.	Fills in: identity of borrower, amount of fine owed, reason for debt, and date.
6		⬠	3.	To registration file.
		○	4.	Attaches slip to reader's registration card.
6	---	⬠	5.	To discharging area.

FLOW PROCESS CHART					SUMMARY			
						Pres. Meth.	Prop. Meth.	Diff.
Subject Charted: _Processing reserves._					Operations			
Present ☐ or Proposed ☒ Method Type of Chart ☒ Man ☐ Product					Transportations			
Chart Begins: _To circulation desk._								
Chart Ends: _Files card in NCF file._					Inspections			
Charted By: _R. Smith_ Date: 5/9-10/1966 Sheet _1_ of _2_					Delays			
					Distance in feet			

Dist. in feet	Time in Min.	Symbol	Step no.	Description of Event
42	---		1.	To circulation desk.
			2.	Picks up accumulation of reserve requests.
			3.	Picks up reserve file.
42			4.	To workroom.
	1.90		5.	Arranges requests into alphabetical order by author.
			6.	Dates reserves if not already dated.
			7.	Checks reserve file to learn if title is already on reserve.
	---		8.	Places request with other requests.
				IF TITLE IS NOT CURRENTLY ON RESERVE
15			1.	To card catalog.
			2.	Checks author-title catalog to learn if book(s) is owned.
300	2.60		3.	To shelves.
25			4.	Checks shelf for title.
			5.	To work area.
			6.	Types a strip for the visible file.
	---		7.	Sets strips on desk.
				IF LIBRARY HAS NOT CATALOGED TITLE REQUESTED
62			1.	To the cataloging room.
	1.10		2.	Searches the processing file.
			3.	Notes on reserve request when a title is on order.
	---		4.	Places a signal flag on the order card.
				IF A BOOK IS CURRENTLY BEING PROCESSED
10			1.	To new book holding shelves.
	.45		2.	Searches for requested title(s).
10			3.	To cataloger's desk.
			4.	Inserts a yellow RUSH slip into each book.

FLOW PROCESS CHART

Subject Charted: Processing reserves.

Present ☐ or Proposed ☒ Method   Type of Chart ☒ Man ☐ Product

Chart Begins: To circulation desk.

Chart Ends: Files card in NCF file.

Charted By: R. Smith   Date: 5/9-10/1966 Sheet 2 of 2

	SUMMARY		
	Pres. Meth.	Prop. Meth.	Diff.
Operations	37	34	3
Transportations	22	13	9
Inspections			
Delays			
Distance in feet	1066	672	394

Dist. in feet	Time in Min.	Symbol	Step no.	Description of Event
62			5.	Places book on desk.
			6.	To workroom.
	---		7.	Files reserve requests.
				IF A BOOK IS NEITHER OWNED NOR ON ORDER

	.29		1.	Files reserves in the Consideration File for the Librarian's attention.

				PREPARING RESERVED BOOKS FOR CIRCULATION
			1.	Pulls drawer of reserves from cabinet.
			2.	Takes requests from file.
			3.	Places cards on desk.
			4.	Writes patron's name and the length of time the title will be held.
			5.	Places card in book.
			6.	Fills out reserve notice to be sent to requester.
	2.16		7.	Places postage stamp on card.
10			8.	To mailbox.
			9.	Drops reserve postals in box.
10			10.	To desk.
			11.	Arranges books alphabetically by patron's name.
			12.	Picks up books and slips for the visible file.
42			13.	To circulation desk.
			14.	Inter-files books with other reserved titles.
	---		15.	Files visible strips.
				PROCESSING "NOT CALLED FOR" RESERVES
42			1.	Removes books from the reserve shelf.
			2.	To workroom.
	1.82		3.	Pulls scratch card from book.
			4.	Records appropriate information on card.
	---		5.	Files card(s) in NCF file.

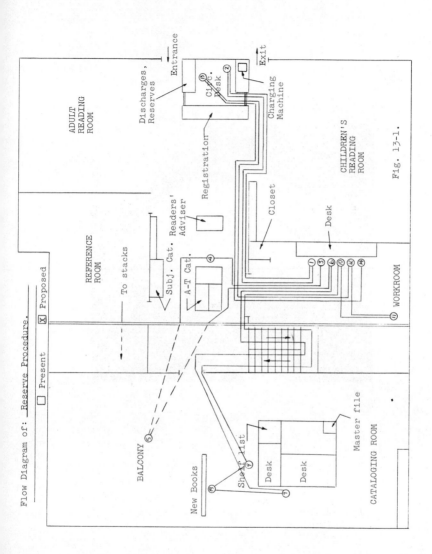

Flow Diagram of: Reserve Procedure.

☐ Present   ☒ Proposed

ADULT READING ROOM

REFERENCE ROOM

BALCONY

New Books

Shelf list

Desk

Desk

CATALOGING ROOM

Master file

To stacks

Subj. Cat.   Readers' Adviser

A-T Cat.

Registration

Discharges, Reserves

Entrance

Circ. Desk

Charging Machine

Exit

Closet

Desk

CHILDREN'S READING ROOM

WORKROOM

Fig. 13-1.

Fig. 13-2

FLOW PROCESS CHART				SUMMARY			
Subject Charted: Sorting transaction cards.					Pres. Meth.	Prop. Meth.	Diff.
Present ☐ or Proposed ☒ Method ǀ Type of Chart ☒ Man ☐ Product				Operations	5	6	-1
Chart Begins: Stacks T-cards as they are received.				Transpor- tations	2	4	-2
Chart Ends: Arranges cards in numerical order.				Inspections			
Charted By: R. Smith Date: 5/16/1966 Sheet 1 of 1				Delays			
				Distance in feet	84	168	-84

Dist. in feet	Time in Min.	Symbol	Step no.	Description of Event
---		◯	1.	Stacks T-cards as they are received.
		◯	2.	Rough sorts cards by series.
		◯	3.	Rough sorts cards by hundreds within series.
42		⇨	4.	To workroom.
		◯	5.	Stores cards in master file.
42	10.53 /100	⇨	6.	To circulation desk.
				SORTING T-CARDS AFTER A SERIES BECOMES TWO WEEKS OVERDUE
42		⇨	1.	To workroom from circulation desk.
		◯	2.	Pulls trays containing cards to be sorted.
42		⇨	3.	To circulation desk
---		◯	4.	Arranges cards in numerical order.
				NOTE: The desk attendants have one week to sort completely one series.

FLOW PROCESS CHART				SUMMARY			
					Pres. Meth.	Prop. Meth.	Diff.
Subject Charted: Processing overdue notices.				Operations			
Present ☐ or Proposed ☒ Method Type of Chart ☒ Man ☐ Product				Transpor-tations			
Chart Begins: Opens notebook.				Inspections			
Chart Ends: Files notices.				Delays			
Charted By: R. Smith Date: 5/18-19/1966 Sheet 1 of 2				Distance in feet			

Dist. in feet	Time in Min.	Symbol	Step no.	Description of Event
---		○	1.	Opens notebook.
6.60 /100		○	2.	Picks up first tray of T-cards.
		○	3.	Sets tray on desk.
		○	4.	Sorts through cards, number by number.
		○	5.	Records missing T-numbers in notebook.
---		○	6.	Returns tray of T-cards to storage case.
				NOTE: Overdue T-cards are placed in a special box daily at the same time the other T-cards are stored.
.39 ---				NOTE: Steps two through six are repeated three times.
.10 ---		○	7.	Checks for recently returned overdue T-cards.
		○	8.	Selects roll of microfilm from cabinet.
		○	9.	Threads film into reader.
.37		○	10.	Turns on machine.
		○	11.	Checks pad for first T-number.
---		○	12.	Searches for corresponding T-number on film.
2.26 ---		○	13.	Types overdue notice.
		○	14.	Records date overdue notice was prepared.
		○	15.	Rewinds film.
		○	16.	Turns off machine.
.17		○	17.	Removes film from machine.
		○	18.	Returns film to cabinet.
---		○	19.	Checks notices against cards in the "red card" file.
		○	20.	Removes throw-away carbons from overdue notices.
		○	21.	Tears off top copy of fanfold.
1.45		○	22.	Folds form in half.
		○	23.	Stuffs notice into window envelope.
		○	24.	Stamps envelope.
---		○	25.	Seals envelope.

FLOW PROCESS CHART					SUMMARY		
						Pres. Meth.	Prop. Meth.	Diff.

Subject Charted: _Processing overdue notices._

Present ☐ or Proposed ☒ Method   Type of Chart ☒ Man ☐ Product

Chart Begins: _Opens notebook._

Chart Ends: _Files notices._

Charted By: R. Smith   Date: 5/18-19/1966 Sheet 2 of 2

	Pres. Meth.	Prop. Meth.	Diff.
Operations	57	54	3
Transpor- tations	33	6	27
Inspections			
Delays			
Distance in feet	1008	108	900

Dist. in feet	Time in Min.	Symbol	Step no.	Description of Event
18	---		26.	To mailbox.
	.26		27.	Drops envelopes into box.
18			28.	To desk.
			29.	Picks up remaining copies of overdue notices.
	---		30.	Files notices.
				SECOND NOTICE
	---		1.	Pulls second notices from file.
	.10		2.	Checks for recently returned overdue T-cards.
	.17		3.	Checks "red card" file.
	1.71		4-14	Repeats steps 20-30 above.
				THIRD NOTICE
	---		1.	Pulls third notices from file.
	.10		2.	Checks for recently returned overdue T-cards.
	---		3.	Checks "red card" file.
	.17			
	1.71		4-14	Repeats steps 20-30 above.

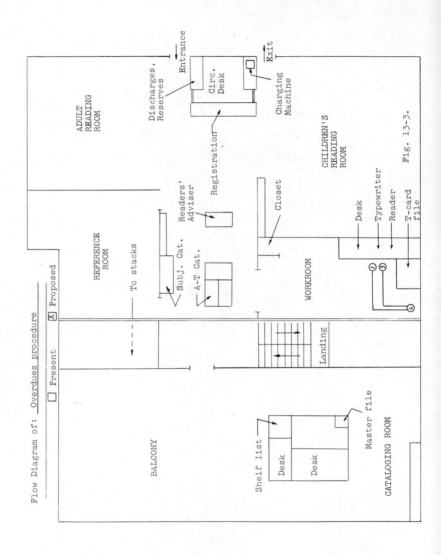

Flow Diagram of: Overdues procedure

☐ Present   ☒ Proposed

Fig. 13-3.

FLOW PROCESS CHART			SUMMARY			
				Pres. Meth.	Prop. Meth.	Diff.
Subject Charted: Recording circulation statistics.			Operations	4	4	0
Present ☐ or Proposed ☒ Method Type of Chart ☒ Man ☐ Product			Transpor- tations	2	2	0
Chart Begins: Picks up circulation statistics book.			Inspections			
Chart Ends: Returns statistics book to desk.			Delays			
Charted By: R. Smith Date: 5/19/1966 Sheet 1 of 1			Distance in feet	12	12	0

Dist. in feet	Time in Min.	Symbol	Step no.	Description of Event
	---		1.	Picks up circulation statistics book.
6			2.	To charging area.
	.70		3.	Checks to determine T-number of last book charged to a series.
			4.	Records number of books charged during one week.
6			5.	To registration area.
	---		6.	Returns statistics book to desk.

				FLOW PROCESS CHART		SUMMARY		

FLOW PROCESS CHART

				SUMMARY			
					Pres. Meth.	Prop. Meth.	Diff.
Subject Charted: __Put-away procedures.__				Operations	10	10	0
Present ☐ or Proposed ☒ Method	Type of Chart ☒ Man ☐ Product			Transportations	2	2	0
Chart Begins: __Opens cash drawer.__				Inspections			
Chart Ends: __Takes day's fines to Librarian's office.__				Delays			
Charted By: __R. Smith__ Date: __5/20/1966__ Sheet __1__ of __1__				Distance in feet	117	117	0

Dist. in feet	Time in Min.	Symbol	Step no.	Description of Event
	---		1.	Opens cash drawer.
			2.	Picks up cash tray.
	13.00		3.	Sits down at desk.
			4.	Counts money.
			5.	Adds total fines recorded on tally slip.
			6.	Reconciles two balances.
	---		7.	Places change in cash drawer for next day's use.
			8.	Places receipts in cash bag.
42			9.	To safe with cash tray and bag.
	.88		10.	Places cash drawer in safe.
			11.	Locks safe.
75	---		12.	Takes day's fines to Librarian's office.

| SUMMARY OF FLOW PROCESS CHARTS | | | | | | | | | | | | | | |
| Present Method | | | | | Proposed Method | | | | | Difference | | | | |
Procedure	○	▷	□	▽	D.T.	○	▷	□	▽	D.T.	○	▷	□	▽	D.T.
Make-ready	17	2	1	-	48	17	2	1	-	48	-	-	-	-	--
Book Prep.	18	5	1	-	60	14	1	1	-	20	4	4	-	-	40
Registration	19	3	3	1	27	7	2	2	-	24	12	1	1	1	3
Charging	24	-	1	-	--	24	-	1	-	--	-	-	-	-	--
Discharging	12	2	1	-	12	12	2	1	-	12	-	-	-	-	--
Reserves	37	22	-	-	1066	34	13	-	-	672	3	9	-	-	394
Sorting T-cards	5	2	-	-	84	6	4	-	-	168	-1	-2	-	-	-84
Overdues	57	33	-	-	1008	54	6	-	-	108	3	27	-	-	900
Renewals	6	-	-	1	--	-	-	-	-	--	6	-	1	-	--
Statistics	4	2	-	-	12	4	2	-	-	12	-	-	-	-	--
Put-away	10	2	-	-	117	10	2	-	-	117	-	-	-	-	--
TOTALS	209	73	7	2	2434	182	34	6	-	1181	27	39	2	1	1253

Fig. 13-4   Summary of flow process charts.

Cost of the Proposed Method

Now that all procedures have been analyzed and improved we are ready to make the time and cost study of the proposed method. The goal will be to arrive at a systems unit cost--that is, the cost of circulating one book. (In an actual situation the time and cost data would probably have been interwoven into the preceding recommendations; but for purposes of illustration they will here be kept separate.) The methodology for conducting a time study has been outlined in Chapter VII. Cost analysis has been discussed in Chapter X. In this chapter we will confine ourselves to a summary accompanied by a few necessary explanations.

Labor Cost

The time data and labor cost are combined in Figure 13-5. The figure includes observed time (T_o), normal or rated time (T_n), and standard time (T_s). For each operation the standard time is multiplied by the average cost per productive hour, which yields the total cost for the year. These individual costs are then summed, giving a total annual labor cost of $9,560.88.

To calculate the average hourly labor charge for circulation, it is not enough merely to divide total labor cost for the year by the total number of hours devoted to circulation. The reason is that persons performing the circulation tasks do not all receive the same salary. The computation must take this fact into account. The details are presented below:

1. Salary Ranges of Library Job Classes:

A.   Senior Clerk $3940-4990 $\overline{x}$ = $4465

B.   Junior Clerk $3340-4180 $\overline{x}$ = $3760

C.   Page $1 per hour.

(For this study, we have selected the average salary $(\overline{x})$ within each range. This figure was chosen because staff salaries are spread evenly from the lower to upper range of the salary scale. If we had been studying a library where most of the salaries were grouped at either the upper or the lower end of the scale, a different average cost would have been selected.)

2. An Average Productive Hour Wage for Each Classification:

A.   Senior Clerk

$4465. 00   Average annual salary.

Additional costs:

161. 86   Library's Social Security Contribution
($4465. 00 x 0. 03625).

89. 30   Library's Contribution to Employee's Retirement Fund ($4465. 00 x 0. 02).

$4716. 16   Senior Clerk's Total Annual Cost to the Library

The normal work week is 38 hours. If the Clerk had no
time off, he would work 52 x 38 hours or 1976 hours per
year. However, the Senior Clerk does have time off. To
obtain productive-time cost we must subtract hours not
worked from 1976 hours. Rest and personal allowances are
already built into the times in Figure 13-4. The following
hours must be subtracted:

76 hours   Two Weeks Vacation (2 x 38 hours)

68 hours   Nine Holidays a Year. 38 hours/5days = 7. 6
hours worked per day on the average.
7. 6 hours x 9 = 68 hours.

38 hours   Sick leave. Ten days per year are permitted, but an average of only five days or
one week per year are actually used.

182 hours   Total Annual Non-Productive Hours

1976 hours minus 182 hours - 1794 productive hours per
year (excluding Rest and Personal allowances)

Labor Cost per   =   Salary Cost + Additional Cost
Productive hour   No. of hrs. actually devoted to productive work.

= $4716. 16
    1794

= $ 2. 63 per hour.

B. Junior Clerk

$ 3760. 00   Average Annual Salary

Additional costs

136. 30   Social Security ($3760. 00 x 0. 03625).

75. 20   Retirement ($3760. 00 x 0. 02).

$3971. 50   Junior Clerk's Total Annual Cost to the Library

As for the Senior Clerk, 182 non-productive hours must be
subtracted from 1976 total hours, giving a remainder of
1794 productive hours per year (excluding Rest and Personal allowances).

Labor Cost per = $3971. 50
Productive hr.   1794

        = $2. 21

C. Page

Labor Cost per = $1. 00 per hour + $0. 0365 Social
Productive hr.   Security.

        = $1. 0365

Pages receive Rest and Personal allowances, but this is
taken into account in the standard time.

3. Amount of Work Performed by Each Classification:

A. . Twenty-two per cent of the circulation work is per-
     formed by Senior Clerks.

B.   Sixty-four per cent of the circulation work is per-
     formed by Junior Clerks.

C.   Fourteen per cent is performed by Pages.

(These figures were arrived at through observation, and examination of job descriptions and work scheduling charts.   They undoubtedly incorporate some error, and should therefore not be
viewed as absolute.)

4. Average Productive Hour Labor Charge for the Circulation System.

Average hourly labor   % of work performed by Senior Clerks
charge for the circula- = x average hourly wage of Senior Clerks
tion system.   One hundred per cent

                              % of work performed by Junior Clerks
                          + x average hourly wage of Junior Clerks
                                  One hundred per cent

                              % of work performed by Pages x aver-
                          +   age hourly wage of Pages.
                                  One hundred per cent

                          =   22 x $2. 63 + 64 x $2. 21 + 14 x $1. 0365
                                              100

                          = $57. 86 + $141. 44 + $14. 51
                                          100

                          = $2. 14 per hour

(The above formula is an example of a weighed mean.   This
technique is used to insure that no one factor will bias the final answer.   For a more detailed discussion of weighed means, the
reader may consult a basic statistics text such as: Freund, John

Measured Elements	T_0 MIN. ×	T_N MIN. × (1.20)	T_S MIN. × (1.14)	Cycles/ YEAR ×	= MIN/ YEAR $\left(\frac{1\,HR}{60\,MIN}\right)^a$ = HRS/ YR (2.14)	× $\frac{COST}{YR}$ = LABOR CHARGE/ YEAR
Make-ready:						
Cash from safe[b]	1.32	1.58	1.80	303	545	9.08	$19.43
Changing date	.26	.31	.35	303	106	1.77	3.78
Dating T-cards	3.26	3.91	4.46	2184	9740	162.33	347.39
Stamping make-ready and put-away	.31/100	.37/100	.42/100	52	22	.37	.79
Book Preparation:						
Book slips	1.33	1.60	1.82	6150	11193	186.55	399.22
Accessioning	.53	.64	.72	6150	4428	73.80	157.93
Book pockets	1.22	1.46	1.66	6150	10209	170.15	364.12
Plastic jackets	2.37	2.84	3.23	4800	15504	258.84	553.92
Transportation[b]	.27	.32	.36	230	82	1.37	2.93
Registration:	1.35	1.62	1.85	5317	9836	163.93	350.81
Charging:						
First book	.15	.18	.21	141700	29757	496.00	1061.41
All others	.14	.17	.19	76300	14497	241.62	517.07
Discharging:						
Checking-in	.10	.12	.14	218000	30520	508.66	1088.53
Overdue fines	.58	.70	.79	12920	10206	170.10	364.01
Delinquent file	1.34	1.60	1.82	160	291	4.85	10.38
Reserves:						
On reserve	1.90	2.28	2.59	2428	6288	104.80	224.27
Owned, not on reserve	2.60	3.12	3.55	1669	5924	98.73	211.28
Title on order	1.10	1.32	1.50	455	682	11.37	24.33
In process	.45	.54	.61	203	123	2.00	4.28
Not owned, on order	.29	.34	.38	304	115	1.91	4.09
Prep. for circ.	2.16	2.59	2.95	4745	13997	233.28	499.22
"NCR" reserves	1.82	2.18	2.48	711	1763	29.38	62.87
Sorting T-cards:	10.53/100	12.63/100	14.40/100	218000	31392	523.20	1119.65
Overdues:						
Checking and recording T-cards	6.60/100	7.92/100	9.03/100	218000	19685	327.63	701.13
Storing T-cards[b]	.39	.47	.54	230	124	2.07	4.43
Reading film	.37	.44	.50	9180	4590	76.51	163.73
Typing notices	2.26	2.71	3.09	4900	15141	252.35	540.03
"Red" card file	.17	.20	.23	960	220	3.68	7.87
Overdue T-card file	.10	.12	.14	3200	448	7.46	15.96
Prep. for mailing	1.45	1.74	1.98	7453	14756	245.93	526.29
Mailing[b]	.26	.31	.35	230	80	1.34	2.87
Circ. statistics:	.70	.84	.96	52	50	.83	1.78
Put-away:						
Bookkeeping	13.00	15.60	17.78	303	5387	89.78	192.13
Cash into safe	.88	1.05	1.20	303	363	6.05	12.95

[a] conversion factor: minutes to hours.
[b] number of workdays 303

TOTAL $9560.88

Fig. 13-5 Time data plus labor charges.

Item	Cost/ item	Cost/ 1000 items	qt./ year	Cost/ year
Plastic jackets		$60.80	6,150	$373.92
Bookslips		2.80	6,150	17.22
Book pockets		6.40	6,150	39.36
Borrowers cards		6.50	3,776	24.54
Juvenile cards		5.85	1,541	9.01
Film		1.44	218,000	313.92
Overdue notices		45.00	4,900	220.50
Paste	$3.08/ gal.		6,000	18.48
Reserve applications		5.20	5,059	26.30
Strips for vis. file		19.00	2,317	44.02
Postage stamps		50.00	7,453	372.65
Window envelopes		11.35	7,453	84.59
Miscellaneous:				50.00[a]
Pencils				
Scratch pads				
Ink pads				
Date stamps				
Unnumbered T-cards				
			TOTAL	$1,594.51

or ... *x* (column operators between headers)

Fig. 13-6 Material costs.

Item	Initial cost[b]	Amortization % [c]	Amortized cost/yr.	Annual serv. charge	Total annual cost
Remington Rand Champion Microfilmer	1310.00	.10	131.00	110.00	$241.00
Microfilm reader	350.00	.10	35.00	25.00	60.00
T-cards (reusable for about ten years)	390.00	.10	39.00		39.00
			TOTAL	$	340.00

Fig. 13-7 Equipment costs.

[a] Estimated cost per year.
[b] Assumed that the equipment will have no salvage value.
[c] Equipment amortized over ten years; straight-line method.

Item	Total Annual Cost
Building Depreciation	$ 2,320[a]
Janitor Service (Including Salaries)	16,072
Building Repair, Maintenance, etc.	4,800
Utilities (Light, Heat, Water and Gas, Telephone)	9,895
Insurance	910

Total General Cost	33,997
Area Used for Circulation	445 sq. ft.[b]
Total Area in Building	14,079 sq. ft.
Percentage of Cost Properly Charged to Circulation	3.16% (445/14,079)[c]

General Cost to be Charged to   =   Total General Cost   x
Circulation   0.0316
                                     = $33,997 x 0.0316
                                     = $1,074

[a] Depreciated in equal increments over 50 years. Original cost=50 x $2,320 or $116,000. Of course if the depreciation were based on current replacement cost, it would be much higher. See Chapter X.

[b] 194 sq. ft. for the circulation desk area + 150 sq. ft. workroom area for reserves and overdues + 100 sq. ft. for book preparation = 445 sq. ft.

[c] Although for convenience utilities are prorated here on the basis of square feet, there are probably more accurate bases for the allocation of some of them. See Chapter X.

Fig. 13-8 General costs.

E. , <u>Modern Elementary Statistics</u>. 2nd ed. Englewood Cliffs,
N. J. , Prentice-Hall, 1960. "The Weighted Mean," p. 67-69.).

Material, Equipment and General Costs

> These costs are presented in Figures 13-6, 13-7, and 13-8
> respectively.

Total Systems Cost

> The total cost is obtained by summing the Labor, Material,
> Equipment, and General Costs:

Labor	$ 9,560.88	(Figure 13-5).
Material	1,594.51	(Figure 13-6).
Equipment	340.00	(Figure 13-7).
General	1,074.00	(Figure 13-8).
	$12,569.39	Total Cost per Year

The Systems Unit Cost

The systems unit cost is found by dividing the total yearly
cost by the number of volumes borrowed per year.   There are
about 218,000 books circulated annually; $12,569.39/218,000 yields
a cost per volume circulated of $0.058.   This cost compares
favorably with the published figures of other systems.   The present
system should, from all indications, be capable of handling much
larger volumes of work without undue strain.

It should be remembered that the systems unit cost represents the time actually required to perform a job.   If work is
scheduled so that there is a substantial amount of employee idle
time, then the actual cost of circulating a book will be higher than
the systems unit cost.   In comparing unit costs from library to
library it will be necessary to determine whether the figures are
computed on the same basis.

Index

either-or sample size, 131-2, 148

required sample size, 126-7, 148-9

Gang process chart see Multiple activity chart.

Gantt, Henry, 15

General cost:
allocation, 162-3
Philadelphia office buildings, 163-4

Gilbreth, Frank B., and Lillian, 15, 40, 70, 78

Hand movements, 66, 70

Hathaway, Horace, 15

Hawthorne experiments, 14

Human relations, 30-32, 81-2

Hundredths of a minute to seconds,
conversion, 100-1

Idle time:
machine, 76
worker, 76

Improved method see Proposed method.

Incentives, wage, 14

Index, left and right, of slide rule, 143-4

Inspection, program of, 179-80

Internal Revenue Service, 159-60

Jigs and fixtures, 70, 72-4

Job classification, 17-8

Job rhythm, 32-33, 70, 74

Jobs:
frequently performed, 22-3
high cost, 24
repetitious, 23
requiring frequent movement, 23
security, 31

Labor cost, 151-3

Labor unions, 14, 18-9

Layout, floor space, 23

Left- and right-hand chart see Operation chart.

Machines, library, 76

Maintenance of equipment, cost, 160

Make-ready operations, 25

Man-machine chart:
definition, 76

Management study, data, gathering, 26

Management study, definition of the problem, 24-6

Management study, importance, 21

Management study, present method, 26-7, 45-8

Management study, proposed method, design of see Proposed method, design

Management study, selection of an area for study:
bottlenecks, 24
frequently performed jobs, 22-3, 66
high cost operations, 24
movement of people or equipment, 23
repetitious jobs, 23

Management study, who should make:
business consultant, 21-2
librarian, 22

Manuals, procedure, 54

Maximum working area, 70-2

Memomotion see Form process chart.

Micromotion study, 15
definition, 76-8
uses, 78

Motion economy, principles, 70-5

Motion picture camera, uses of, 76-8

Motion study, definition of, 26

Motions:
arm, 70-2

Motivation, worker 1A3

Multi-part forms, 6G2

Multiple-activity chart:
definition, 76
moving books (illus.) 76
uses, 76

Multiplication:
checking, 139